We Bel[ong to]
the Land

The *Erma Konya Kess*
LIVES OF THE JUST AND VIRTUOUS SERIES

The University of Notre Dame Press gratefully acknowledges the generous support of the estate of Erma Konya Kess in the publication of this series.

We Belong to the Land

THE STORY OF A PALESTINIAN ISRAELI
WHO LIVES FOR PEACE AND
RECONCILIATION

Elias Chacour
with Mary E. Jensen

WITH A NEW PREFACE
BY ELIAS CHACOUR

University of Notre Dame Press
Notre Dame, Indiana

Manufactured in the United States of America

Library of Congress Cataloging-in-Publication Data

Chacour, Elias, 1939–
We belong to the land.
p.   cm. — (Erma Konya Kess lives of the just and virtuous series)
Includes bibliographical references.
ISBN 0-268-01963-0 (pbk. : alk. paper)
1. Chacour, Elias, 1939–   2. Palestinian Arabs—Israel—
Galilee—Biography.   3. Catholic Church—Byzantine rite,
Melchite—Israel—Galilee—Clergy—Biography.   4. Arab-Israeli
conflict.   I. Series.

DS113.7 .C495 2001
956.94'0049274'0092—dc21
[B]   00-052773

∞ *This book is printed on acid-free paper.*

To all who have formed my personality as a priest,
who have encouraged me in my task
through their love and understanding,
and who have shared my mission and work.

Contents

CONTENTS

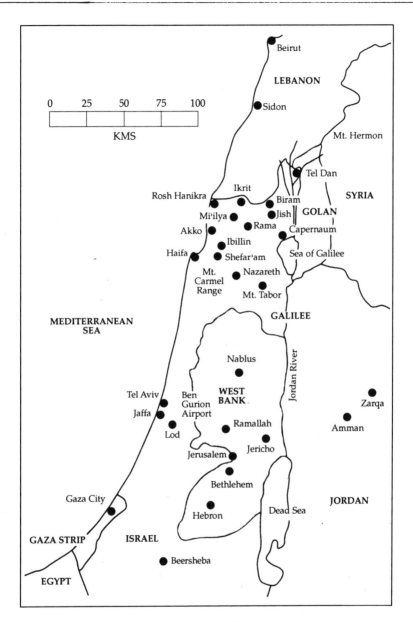

Map of Israel

Preface to the New Edition

"For every tree is known by its own fruits. For of thorns men do not gather figs, nor from a bramble bush gather they grapes."

Luke 6:44

Good trees give good fruit.

What has become of the Prophet Elias High School in Ibillin, Galilee, Israel? What has Abuna Chacour become after all these years? *We Belong to the Land* ended at the dawn of 1991. One building stood alone on the Mount of Light, a high school for approximately 800 students. Since then we have progressed enormously. The present campus enrollment is approximately 4,000 students and 275 faculty members. They commute every morning from seventy different villages and towns all over Israel. In any given week more than 4,000 *Children of God* come to Mar Elias Educational Institutions. They generously radiate joy and take back home with them friendship, hope and knowledge.

We have grown so much. The school became the "Mar Elias Educational Institutions" (MEEI). This is the only Arab campus in all of Israel and the high school is only one part of this campus. We have added the College with its three-year program following high school and have started working toward accreditation as a full-fledged university.

Nineteen hundred and ninety-four was a year of challenge at Mar Elias. We felt the urgency of providing an alternative that would slow down the rate of emigration from the Holy Land,

xi

especially of the Christian Palestinians. Many more Palestinian Christians live in the huge Diaspora of the Western world than in the Holy Land itself. We reached the conclusion that the only thing that could slow down this tragic emigration would be the creation of an Arab-Christian-Israeli university. No one except us, a small group of believers and friends, were ready to consider this possibility. It would cost millions and no one had the funds. Besides, who could deal with the civil and religious authorities to get their blessing and endorsement for the project? Many of the Arab citizens in Israel realize that we cannot hope for any blessing from the authorities, since in fact they have no blessing to give.

We had no choice but to fall back on the popular adage: *"It is easier to seek forgiveness than to obtain permission."* Once again we sought to establish an accomplished fact.

What was going on there on the Mount of Light on that morning of October 14, 1994? University students at Mar Elias? Yes! One hundred students were gathered in the gymnasium. They looked lost inside the big hall. I began my opening speech. Here are some of my remarks:

"My friends, today at this moment we are starting a new page in the history of Israel-Palestine. We are challenging everyone in this country. We are ready for the long march toward the first Christian-Arab-Israeli university. We have matured and we refuse to be dependent on others for our education. Our community is ready to take the initiative. We want to build this country together with our Jewish brothers and sisters. It is time to challenge them all with higher education and modern skills. We have conformed long enough to the type of "good citizen" they imposed on us. We refuse any more to be passive. We want to build this country together. We need to be genuine, active citizens, to be partners in the decision-making process. We have to start now, together with our Jewish brothers and sisters, to prepare the future we want for our children. Both the Jews and Palestinians are children of Abraham. The Gentile Friend of God, *Khalilu Allah*, is our common father. They the Jews and we the Palestinians can never be a sign of hope for the nations unless we reconcile and give a joint witness of compassion and of mercy. Through your presence you become a **living stone**. Together you are the cornerstone of this future university.

"You must know that we decided to start without any kind of permit. We have permits neither from the Church, nor from the academic or civil authorities. We do not have permission to open

xii

the first scholastic year, but we have the God-given right to education and no one can deprive us. You want a university! You have decided to join us in the long march! You are ready to take the risk, to get your hands dirty. That is why you are here.

"It is time for us to proclaim loud and clear this is the hour to create an institution of higher education inside the state of Israel, an Arab-Israeli university. We want Jewish students to come and join us. They will not be considered guests or a minority. They are invited to be our partners, part of our own self. We need their presence and their help, but we are also ready to share with them and to offer them help. We are citizens of this big national community and want to be active citizens. Bear with us all the problems and the difficulties. We will not rest until we have the recognition of the authorities and accreditation from the educational institutions. Through perseverance we can overcome.

"We need to challenge the authorities with perseverance, excellence in achievement, and the highest possible standard of human values. There will be moments of hardship, of despair, of doubt, of temptation to give up, times when we long to turn and go home. I invite you, every time you reach the bottom of hope, to start again beyond despair. To sink into despair is not for us. Out from the tomb comes the Resurrection. Isn't it true that the Friday of the crucifixion is followed by the Sunday of the Resurrection? Yes, my dear friends, it is the reality. Those who *sow with tears shall reap with joy.*

"I close my eyes and look three years ahead. You shall not be alone, you shall double, even triple in number. You shall be hundreds and thousands to start the school year. You shall not remain alone—Christians, Moslem and Druze. Keep a place ready for our Jewish brothers and sisters. They will be missed always until they come and sit with us around these simple desks. They will come and start the serious work of preparing together the future we all want for our children. Now, my dear friends, thank you for the immense trust you put in each other. Together we have no other way but to be stronger than any possible misunderstanding or any storm that might arise on our way toward our common goal; the Arab-Christian-Israeli university in Galilee . . ."

The college opened in October 1994. The facilities were in use from 8 am until 9 pm. Not a single classroom went unused during the daytime, so we ran two shifts, one for the high school, the other for the college.

We found it necessary to add at least a hundred new classrooms. We decided not to accept any fund raising from big organizations that would enslave us. Rather, we would continue to rely on the small means we had and the many friends who believed in what we were doing. When we began the new building, out of nowhere friends responded to our appeal. Their small donations were most effective.

We shall never forget the magnificent letter we received at the beginning of 1997 from an elderly American lady. She wrote, "Father Chacour, I read your books, I follow you from afar as much as I can. You have changed my life to the extent that I identify with what you are doing. Through what you are doing you embody forgiveness, courage, and determination. You surely learned the lesson from the One you call '*My Compatriot.*' I decided to send you for the new building all my savings from last month." Inside her letter was a check for ten American dollars. This donation was worth so much more than the ten dollars. A classroom in the new building has been named after that beautiful child of God who sent us "all her savings from last month." I pray that God blesses her with a long life and many months to save ten more dollars and to rejoice in giving away what she has saved.

The thousands of visitors who have come to Mar Elias College during these past years have made the dream become a reality. Their presence and their solidarity strengthen our weakness and fill us with courage. It is like living a dream. Every morning thousands of children of God climb the Mountain of Light; Moslems, Druze, Jews and Christians alike. They arrive with a beautiful smile on their faces, as if saying "*we've come home.*" Mar Elias is our college. We have a future. We have hope. The college is a great success. It has the support of the Arab minority inside Israel and of so many Jews as well. The first year enrollment was 100 students, then 340, 550, 740 and 800 students. At the end of the second scholastic year we had already won the sympathy of the authorities. Then Foreign Minister Shimon Peres came to the school to see what was going on in that remote place called Ibillin. He said that he had come to the school to see with his own eyes what visiting U.S. Secretary of State James Baker had raised so much concern about in Jerusalem. It was indeed due to Baker's strong intervention that we received the building permit for the gymnasium.

Peres proposed to be our ambassador from that time on. He encouraged the Minister of Education, Professor Rubenstein, to visit. This man came with a priceless gift, a gift for which we had waited a long time . . . he came to officially recognize the existence of the college and to give us accreditation. What a victory that was! It was a victory for the minister himself, for the Jewish people, for the Palestinians, and especially for our students. We had won the trust and the friendship of the Ministry of Education and the Ministry of Labor. Furthermore, Mar Elias College was awarded the "Certificate of Excellence" among all Israeli Colleges in the years 1998 and 1999.

Since 1991 we have lived through intense moments of sadness and of fear, mainly during the Gulf War. We experienced the shock of real terrorism from both Israeli and Palestinian individuals. We always try to protest against the prevailing violence. No matter who; no matter against whom; violence breeds violence. We cannot expect peace to come out of violence. You know the tree from its fruit.

Two important days in the short history of the college shall remain always rooted in our minds. The first? After the atrocious suicidal bombing in Tel Aviv our students decided to donate blood for the injured Jews in Tel Aviv . . . 300 out of 350 students donated blood to the victims of terror. Palestinian blood started flowing into Jewish veins, restoring life where life was meant to be destroyed. We are an institution created mainly to fill the minds of our students with science and knowledge, but we also want to give them new dimensions of ethics and of generosity.

I shall never forget the scene of the fifteen Jewish nurses taking our Arab Palestinian blood to infuse into the veins of our Jewish brothers and sisters lying in the hospitals of Tel Aviv. As we donated the blood, lying on the bed next to me was a teacher from our Jewish faculty, beside her a Druze teacher, and beside him an American volunteer working as my administrative secretary.

The second great day was the visit of former Secretary of State, James Baker. As I previously mentioned, James Baker did everything possible to obtain the building permit for our gym. The Bakers honored us with their visit to Mar Elias College and agreed to dedicate the new library building.

Mar Elias College became a pilgrimage place for people looking for inspiration and for hope. Among those thousands who came were students from Grosse Pointe Memorial Presbyterian Church, from Christ Church, Sacramento, and the beautiful Volunteers in Mission, young and old, who got their hands dirty helping to build the campus. May they know that the dirt on their hands has been a great blessing for us.

This story of Mar Elias is not yet at its end. We are just beginning. Our hopes go far beyond what has been achieved. Our next five-year plan, the strategic plan of our directors, is to welcome 5,000 students by the year 2005. Will you be a part of the adventure? Here is our address:

Mar Elias Educational Institutions
P.O. Box 102, Ibillin
Galilee, 30012
Israel.

Come and get your hands dirty with us.

Chapter 1

Stronger Than the Storm

"Your passport," the Israeli policewoman demanded, holding out her hand. In the midst of all the international passengers waiting to have their luggage inspected at Ben Gurion Airport, she had approached me. I gave her my well-worn Israeli passport.

"You are Arab?" she asked, glancing at the document.

"Not only Arab, but also I am Palestinian." The Israeli government and many Jewish Israelis choose not to acknowledge the existence of Palestinian people, preferring to categorize them with all other people who speak Arabic.

"Take your suitcase and follow me," the policewoman ordered, and began threading her way through the masses of passengers and luggage.

Every time I need to travel in or out of Israel I have the same experience. Palestinian people, whether Israeli citizens or residents of Occupied Palestine, are automatically subjected to private and often rigorous questioning and inspection. They are considered dangerous, a threat to the security of Israel and to travel safety. Security measures are important for all of us, but it is wrong when one group of people is systematically harassed and humiliated in the process. On this spring day in 1985 I needed to be in London for a television interview, but I knew I might be denied permission to leave the country.

Finally we arrived at a separate corner of the airport, where other Palestinian people were already waiting. An older couple stood near their suitcases, which were open on a table. Israeli policewomen examined each item, patting and shaking sweaters, socks, and undergarments to loosen anything hidden. The

Palestinian woman, in her beautifully embroidered dress, was quickly collecting her private garments, trying to shield them from further invasion. She kept her head bowed, her face nearly hidden in the folds of her long, white head scarf. Her husband's face was set in a scowl beneath his white *keffiyeh*, the Arab headdress. He tried to keep his belongings together as they were stacked on the table.

A muscular young Palestinian man dressed in a business suit was ordered to enter a small cubicle. He might have been a teacher or a lawyer. As he moved toward the cubicle, I saw deep pain and humiliation in his eyes. He would be required to strip off his clothes, allowing the police to carefully inspect his whole body. Most likely he would also have to endure a body cavity search. The stated reasons for such indignity are airline safety and the security of Israel, but Palestinians know the treatment is intended to humiliate their pride and their soul. The young man entered the cubicle, and the door was closed. No one spoke. Tension, anger, and hopelessness hung heavily all about us. The policewomen were now examining the older couple's luggage itself. Soon they, too, would go into separate cubicles for a body search.

"What's your name?" I asked, speaking in Hebrew to the policewoman who had brought me here.

"Mikki," she answered, regarding me carefully. She saw a priest with black hair, olive-colored skin, and a full black beard richly streaked with gray, searching her own face with his intense brown eyes behind gold-rimmed glasses.

"Mikki, do you know what we Palestinians will say to each other when we are released from here? We will look at each other very sadly and say, 'These poor Jewish police need to humiliate us to feel that they are powerful and secure. They are teaching us to hate them, but we shall not learn the lesson.' Do you know why?"

She stared at me, transfixed, and almost imperceptibly shook her head.

"Because hatred is corruption, Mikki, and we refuse to be corrupted by hatred. We will not react to what you do to us with the same treatment. We will act genuinely to find a way to liberate ourselves from this humiliation. You have known what it means to be oppressed and persecuted, but you have forgotten too quickly."

"It is not good to be naive," the policewoman said, wrenching her gaze from my eyes and turning away, but not before I had seen her tears.

"You have not been naive or weak, Mikki. You have rather been transparent, sincere, and human. I thank you for these feelings. Whenever you come to Galilee, come and visit me. I'll be very happy to receive you."

"I am really sorry," the policewoman said, "but I had to give your passport to my boss. I cannot take you back to the other passengers now."

"That's fine. Do not let me go."

A few moments later a stocky, blond policeman arrived, holding my passport in his hand. "What is your name?" he demanded.

The strident, arrogant tone of his voice chilled me to the bone. I could hear echoes of the Jewish Zionist soldiers who had ordered me, my family, and all the villagers out of our homes in Biram, far north in Galilee, when I was eight years old. The tone implied "dirty, dangerous Palestinian who does not count as a human being." Today we Palestinians are considered dirty and dangerous, just as this policeman's father was called "dirty Jew" only some forty years ago.

"My name is written on my passport. My passport is in your hands."

"I don't read English."

"It is written in Hebrew."

All activity had stopped in the small corner. Palestinians and police alike were frozen in place.

The policeman regarded me with even more hostility, speaking slowly and distinctly. "I want to hear that from your mouth."

"Fine. I am Abuna Elias Chacour." *Abuna* literally means "our father" and is the Arabic title for a priest.

"What is the name of your father?"

"My father is Mikhail." Father's kind and gentle face flashed before my eyes. *This man is a child of God,* Father would say. *He is not aware of his self-defeating arrogance. Love him.*

3

"Where were you born?"

"In Biram." I sensed a slight movement among the people. The tragic story of the villages of Biram and Ikrit and the struggles of their residents to return are well known in Israel and Occupied Palestine.

"Your father—where was he born?"

"In Biram." *God, help me to love this man, but give me wisdom to speak the truth also.*

"Your grandfather?"

"In Biram."

"To which generation can you go back in Biram?" Tapping my passport against his fingers, the policeman spoke with mock patience and courtesy.

My chin jutted out, which caused my beard to point almost directly at the policeman's face. This was no longer a matter of checking security. "Let me tell you a story," I said in a voice loud enough to allow everyone in the corner to hear.

"One of my forefathers was sitting under our fig tree in front of our house one day. He was eating figs and enjoying God's gift to him in the land of his ancestors. Suddenly he saw down the path a poor stranger, a foreigner who was poorly dressed. His feet were bare, he was covered with dust, and he was tired, hungry, and thirsty. He looked scared. My forefather called to him. The stranger came. He was given food to eat, water to drink, clothes to wear, and a place to rest."

The policeman tapped his foot impatiently on the floor. The Palestinians seemed to hold their breath. All inspection work was forgotten.

"And then, after the foreigner was rested and about to leave, my ancestor asked him his name. He discovered that that foreigner was *your* forefather Abraham, coming from Iraq, Mesopotamia, a Gentile among a Gentile nation."

A collective sigh escaped from the Palestinians. The words expressed every Palestinian's knowledge and belief: we belong to the land and our ancestors have been in the land of Palestine for thousands of years. The young state of Israel cannot change that.

"Take your luggage and go away!" the policeman shouted. "I don't want to see you here."

"Yes, sir. Goodbye." I picked up my suitcase and walked to my plane, hoping and praying that the other Palestinians would not suffer because of my words.

I settled into my window seat on the London-bound plane and gratefully closed my eyes. I had left my village, Ibillin, very early because I had wanted to visit my father in Haifa on my way to the airport. He was eighty-seven years old, still in good health but growing frail. Father, or Abu Rudah (father of Rudah, his oldest son), had been in my sister Wardi's little garden when I arrived.

"How are you, Father?"

"I'm well, praise to God." Father's *keffiyeh* protected his eyes from the early morning sun. He looked just the way I remembered him from my earliest childhood, only with more wrinkles on that wonderful face. "And you, my son? How are you?"

"I am fine, Father. I am very busy in Ibillin and am traveling outside the country, too. In fact, I am on my way to the airport to fly to London. I'm going to be on television later this evening." I told Father about the ten-part British television series entitled "The Gods of War." I had been invited to speak about "The God of Love."

Father's eyes brightened. "That's excellent! You have a chance to tell many people about God's love in Jesus, our Compatriot from Galilee. And don't forget the tragedy of Biram. Tell everyone that we, the people of Biram, are still alive and we want to go back to our home."

"Yes, Father, I will tell them."

Father poked at a tilting tomato plant with his walking stick, then glanced up at me. "I have been wondering if you have any news about Biram. Will the government allow us to go back soon? Will they help us rebuild our houses and regain our olive and fig trees? Will I be able to die in Biram where I was born?"

Sighing and shaking my head, I enfolded Father's frail body in my arms. How I wished I could take him back to a rebuilt Biram before I must carry him dead to the village cemetery. In

1948 the Jewish Zionist soldiers had tricked the people of Biram into leaving by telling them about an imaginary attack and giving a worthless written guarantee of return. After two weeks in the nearby fields, we discovered our warm, pleasant village life in Biram was gone forever. The soldiers had ransacked our houses and ruined our food supply. Most of the village men were herded into trucks at gunpoint and driven away. Old people, women, and children were left to fend for themselves. Some fled to Lebanon, others to neighboring villages. My mother, my sister Wardi, my brother Atallah, and I went to Jish, a village only a few kilometers away from Biram. Father and my three oldest brothers finally returned several months later after walking through Jordan, Syria, and Lebanon, slipping back into Galilee to be reunited with us.

"I am sorry, Father," I said as I released him. "The Committee of Biram Refugees is working hard to convince the Israeli government that we should be allowed to reclaim at least part of our land and rebuild Biram, but it is a very difficult and slow process. We have no might in our hands. We only have the right to return, as declared by the courts."

"I know," Father said simply. "I know. But it is better to have the right than the might, because might corrupts. It declares the right to be wrong and the wrong to be right." He reflected a moment, then spoke pensively. "You will take me back to Biram when I die, won't you, my son? I want to be buried where your mother and my ancestors lie sleeping. I want to join them as we await the resurrection."

"Of course, Father. I will take you there myself."

"Good. That's good. But if my fondest wish could be granted, I would go back to Biram alive and rebuild our house, the house I inherited from my forefathers. I would sit under the fig tree in front of our house, and even if it were for only one day, I would die a happy man."

Biram had been an entirely Christian Palestinian village. The Maronite church, grandly named Notre Dame, was the center of our lives. Our school was held in one of the small church buildings. Only about seventy people in the village were Melkite Byzantine Christians (Greek Catholic), including my family. Our bishop had given us into the care of the Maronite priest, Abu Eid. All of us in the village were baptized, married, and buried in that little church, celebrating the liturgy every Sunday and on feast days.

I was four years old and my brother Atallah was six when our parents decided it was time for us to be baptized. Atallah was duly anointed with oil and immersed in the water, but as soon as I was anointed I ran out of the church and hid in the rabbit hole in our woodpile. I did not want to be stripped of my clothes and immersed in water. The afternoon shadows were very long before Mother was finally able to convince me that I was safe from being baptized. For more than a year my family teased that I was half Christian and half nothing. Then one day when I was five years old, I agreed very calmly to be baptized, but without stripping.

Years later, just before I was to be ordained as a deacon at the seminary in Paris, I decided I should tell my dear friend, the seminary superior, about a problem.

"Father Longère, I know it sounds strange, but I must tell you that I have been baptized but never confirmed."

"How come?" he asked in amazement. "This is impossible! You did not receive the Holy Spirit!"

"I have the Holy Spirit, Father," I said, "or the Holy Spirit has me. But I was not confirmed." I told him the whole, long story about Biram and Jish, and how, in the disruption of refugee life, I passed the age of fourteen and never confirmed my baptism.

Father Longère went to the Archbishop of Paris, Cardinal Feltín, and told him the story. Within a few days, Cardinal Feltín himself came and confirmed me. And so I was baptized in a Maronite church, confirmed by a Roman Catholic cardinal, and ordained into the Melkite priesthood.

I slept most of the way to London, awakening only when the flight attendant instructed us to fasten our seat belts for landing. I could see the English coastline and green fields through sporadic clouds. How could this lovely country have ignored the rights and needs of Palestinian people in 1917? I wondered. In that year the Balfour Declaration stated Great Britain's support for a Jewish homeland in Palestine. Although the declaration also stated that the indigenous people should not be deprived of their rights, this was easily ignored and forgotten. The Balfour Declaration was later used to fortify the 1947 United Nations recommendation that Palestine be partitioned between Jews and Palestinians. All of this was decided without consulting us, the Palestinian people, who had been in the land for thousands of years. And the Jewish Zionist soldiers came with guns and forced my family to leave Biram.

In London the BBC television interviewer gave me the opportunity to speak of my Compatriot from Galilee, Jesus Christ, and of the Palestinian people. Finally, at the end of the hour, he posed a fascinating question. "Well, Father Chacour, I wonder, how can you, as a Palestinian Christian Arab, believe in a Jewish Christ?"

I saw the arrogant policeman in the airport. I saw my home village of Biram. I saw the people in my Melkite community in Ibillin. But most of all, I saw Jesus, striding toward me over the Galilee hills, smiling, holding out his hand to me.

"It is as easy for us to believe in our Jewish Christ as it is for Jews to believe in their Iraqi/Mesopotamian, Gentile father, Abraham," I answered. "Abraham never denied that he was a Gentile born among Gentile people—a foreigner, a stranger. But he became a new starting point. If a true sinner, Abraham, an Iraqi Gentile, was able to become a starting point, how much more did my Lord Jesus Christ become something very new, absolutely new, without rejecting the old, but recalling the old to be renewed."

After the interview, I visited with the BBC personnel.

"Where are you from, Father?" a cameraman asked.

"I am from a little village called Ibillin in Israel."

"Is that right? I never heard of it."

"I'm not surprised. Ibillin is on a hill and we can see Mount Carmel, Haifa, Akko, the Mediterranean Sea, and even the Lebanese border."

"It sounds like a real vacation spot, Father!"

I laughed at the thought. Ibillin—a vacation spot? Hardly. But to me there was great beauty in every house, in every yard, in every street. The beauty was in the people. I had not immediately seen that beauty, however, when I arrived in 1965.

Chapter 2

We Don't Want You Here!

"And just where is the village of Ibillin, Bishop Hakim?" I asked. I was sitting in the well-appointed office of the Melkite archbishop of the diocese of Akko, Nazareth, Haifa, and all Galilee, learning about my first assignment as a newly ordained priest.

"Oh, it's not far from here, Elias," the bishop said, waving his hand generally eastward. "Someone can tell you. There's a small Melkite community in Ibillin. But I must be honest; it may not be right for you."

"I am anxious to try, Bishop. I want to start work with my community as soon as possible."

"Just go to Ibillin for one month. Either you like it and you stay, or you don't like it and we'll find another place for you. Remember, Elias, this assignment is only provisionary for a month."

The Melkite church has different names. Some call it the Greek Catholic church, others call it the Uniate church, and we call ourselves the Melkite Catholic church. We are in communion with the Holy See of Rome.

The word *Melkite* originated in the eleventh century when the king of Constantinople allied with the pope in Rome against the patriarch of Constantinople. Those people who followed the king were called "royalists." *Malech* in Arabic gives us the word *Melkite*, which means "royalist," or one who follows the king.

The Melkite Catholic church has the same ancient Byzantine theology, discipline, liturgies, canon laws, and traditions as the Greek Orthodox church.

9

I left Haifa early on the morning of August 15, 1965, to drive to the village of Ibillin. It was the Day of the Assumption of Mary into Heaven, and the Melkite community would expect me to celebrate the liturgy as my first priestly act.

Although Ibillin is only thirty minutes from Haifa, it took me two hours to find it. A hitchhiking soldier directed me toward his own destination in eastern Galilee, pretending it was near Ibillin. Only with the kind help of a petrol station attendant was I able to backtrack and find Ibillin that morning.

Finally I drove up the Ibillin hill on a narrow, stony, winding road between the flat-roofed cement houses and shops. Curious men, women, and children looked at this strange priest in his white Volkswagen slowly bumping through their village. I smiled and waved when I dared take my hands off the steering wheel.

At the top of the hill I found a large stone church standing on a barren plot of land. I parked by a small building next to the church.

"Who are you?" a loud voice demanded. "What do you want?" A frowning man of about forty years was blocking my effort to get out of the car.

"I am Abuna Elias Chacour. I am sent by the bishop to be your priest." Who was this angry man? Why was he talking to me like this?

"I know that he sent you. Go back to him and say that we don't want you."

"But why?"

"You first go and bring what you have stolen from the church and then we will accept you here."

I was flabbergasted. What could this man be talking about? "But, sir, this is the first time I have been in Ibillin. I'm a brand new priest. I have not had time to work or to steal."

"I don't care," the man said, refusing to move. "Go away."

I opened the car door and firmly pushed him aside so I could get out. "Well," I said, "why don't we pray together? Lord, help us to accept each other and not to accuse without assurance of guilt. Help us not to be judges of one another." I then prayed for the community and for the church. When I had finished, the man whom I now realized was the Responsible of the church sighed and relented a little.

"You want to pray? Fine. We are in the church and waiting for you."

Relief washed over me, and I reached for my vestments and small valise in the car.

"But you have a completely empty church," the man said. "The other priest took everything."

The Responsible was right. Except for the old benches and the stone altar, the sanctuary had been stripped of all its furnishings. About fifty men, women, and children silently watched me enter and walk slowly toward the front of the church. These people were my community, the living stones, the family of believers. I nodded at them, trying to smile, but I was frightened. The whole atmosphere was cold and forbidding.

The iconostasis, or wall dividing the altar area from the congregation, was very plain and had three arched doorways. On either side of the largest, middle archway were two icons painted on the wall. On the right was a picture of Jesus, holding the globe in his left hand and raising his right hand in blessing. On the left was a picture of the Virgin Mary, giving her child, Christ, to the world. Through the middle archway I could see the square altar, bare except for the bottle of wine and loaf of bread resting on it.

The entire space behind the iconostasis was empty except for the altar itself. There was no side table for the preparation of bread and wine, no working tables, no candle stands or cross. There were also no curtains to pull in front of the archways. The people watched my every movement as I put on my vestments and said the private prayers with each garment. How long had it been since they had had a priest? I wondered. And was it actually the former priest who had taken all the furnishings? Why hadn't the bishop told me about this? Did the bishop even know about the problems here?

I began to sing the liturgy. Only one old man in the congregation, Abu Jirius, sang the responses. Everyone else just watched and listened. Only a few people came to receive the Eucharist. After the liturgy, the Responsible herded the people

11

out, and I barely had a chance to speak to anyone. They seemed afraid of the angry man.

"I am in charge around here," the Responsible informed me as I repacked my valise. "It is my task to oversee the church and the parish house as well as the pieces of land that the church owns."

"I would like to see the parish house now," I told the Responsible, deciding I would not be intimidated by this man. "I need to get settled so I can begin my work as priest among the people."

The parish house, the small structure alongside the church, was in dreadful condition. Even the doors were missing.

Pointing at the first doorway, the Responsible announced, "That's your bedroom." Stepping inside, I saw a shambles of dirt, trash, and broken furniture on a concrete floor. In one corner was an ancient bed frame with a dirty, deteriorated mattress falling from it. Off to one side was an old desk with junk piled all over it. Broken chairs were scattered about.

"Now I'll show you the kitchen," the Responsible called from outside. Hesitantly I peered into the second, smaller room. Garbage and dirty, crusty dishes and cooking pots were strewn everywhere. A single water tap protruded from the wall. To one side was a very old gasoline engine used for cooking. It was incredibly dirty.

"There is no gas or electricity," the Responsible said, motioning me to come outside. "And there are no toilet facilities." He pointed to a littering of junk a few meters from the parish house. "That used to be a toilet, but the priest brought a bulldozer and leveled it. Then he went away, taking all our church ornaments and furnishings. If you stay, you'll have to manage as best you can. Does it suit you?"

I had never seen such squalor. Biram had been primitive, surely, but had been cared for with love and respect. Now I was fresh from six years in Paris, where as seminarians we had lived like little kings in the beautiful university of St. Sulpice, the Institut Catholique, and the Sorbonne. I had been enjoying Paris. Now it seemed I would have to enjoy the nothingness of this parish house in this village.

"Well?" the Responsible demanded impatiently. "Does this suit you or not?" I knew he was waiting to tell everyone I had failed and gone away.

Goodness, Elias, I said to myself, *it is only for one month. You will manage. You will survive.*

I turned to look at the Responsible, this hard man who was already savoring his victory. "This is fine for me," I replied. "It is good enough. I will stay."

Ibillin. It had been a struggle to find it, and now it was a struggle to stay, I reflected one evening as I paced in the churchyard. I had been in the village almost a month but continued to be largely ignored by the people. Was this due to carelessness or inexperience? I did not know.

The Responsible was harassing me daily about many small things. I knew he was exercising his self-appointed power over me, and although I respected his position, I resented his intrusion into my pastoral work.

The celebrations of the Divine Liturgy were dismal. Only about twenty people attended on Sunday, and when Abu Jirius was not there, I had to sing the entire liturgy alone. Not only was it exhausting for me, but also the people were being deprived of the wholeness of God's blessing. Furthermore, only a handful of people received Holy Communion, and the rest ignored my suggestions that they participate.

I was fighting desperately to adjust to the poor living conditions. The most difficult was the lack of toilet or bathing facilities. The villagers could easily relieve themselves under the trees or behind a rock, but for me it was impossible. I had taken to asking strangers in the village for permission to use their toilet facilities, but it was inconvenient and embarrassing, to say the least.

After cleaning the worst of the garbage and dirt from my bedroom/office and throwing out the unusable bed frame, I had laid the crumbling, dirty mattress directly on the concrete floor. With the two blankets I had brought with me, I managed to make a place where I could lie down. Some nights, however, I gave up on the mat and tried to rest in the backseat of my car. Sleep proved to be impossible because of the hard floor, the cramped quarters of the Volkswagen, the ever-present insects,

13

and my tremendous loneliness and grief. From Paris to Ibillin—it was too big a change for me.

I was also very hungry. As yet I had received no salary from the bishop, and what little money I had brought with me was gone. I had assumed the Melkite community hospitality toward their new priest would include meals, but everyone was ignoring me. Now, during my fourth week in Ibillin, I had eaten substantial meals only twice. Even the remains of the communion bread were gone. I would soon need to start foraging in the fields and orchards.

God, where are you? I demanded angrily. *How could you let me come into such a dreadful situation? Most of the people won't even talk to me. How can I be priest to them, showing your love, your forgiveness, and your care, if I can't communicate with them? How can I work at that communication if I'm not sleeping and not eating, if my poor back and my muscles are constantly aching, and my eyes are burning from petrol fumes and candle smoke, if I'm feeling utterly alone and abandoned in this village?*

I stumbled to the church steps and sat down, laying my arms across my knees and burying my head. *Why doesn't my own bishop express some concern for me? There he is in that comfortable palace in Haifa—and here I am in such misery, trying to be a priest in this place where he sent me.*

Tears poured from my eyes and dampened my thick, black beard. Just two months earlier I had been ordained priest in Nazareth along with Faraj, my classmate and friend. We had met in Haifa at the Bishop's School when we were twelve years old. As we studied in Paris together, we often spoke of how we would live our priesthood, agreeing always that we would never exploit people, never sell the sacraments, and never seek material gain for ourselves. The survival of our church in Palestine was a miracle from God, we knew, and we saw our task as teaching God's love and convincing our people who had been born into their Christianity that it's important to make this Christianity meaningful.

Faraj and I were the first to be ordained priests in the Melkite diocese of Galilee in twenty-six years. In 1947 and 1948 the Christian community was dismantled as Palestinian people became refugees inside Israel and in the surrounding Arab countries. An estimated 390,000 Christians had fled from Galilee in fear, including the Melkite bishop and some of the priests, leaving the remaining Christians in leaderless chaos.[1] After the creation of the state of Israel it was impossible to bring in Arab priests, and we were quite abandoned in our villages. Our ordination was a rebirth of Christian hope in the Holy Land. Bishop Hakim invited all the Melkite Christians in Galilee, the leaders of all the other Christian denominations, and diplomatic officials to attend the ordination in the Greek Catholic seminary church of St. Joseph in Nazareth.

I had had many questions before I was ordained. *Am I making the right decision? Am I worthy of ordination?* At the age of twenty-five I was taking a step that could not be reversed. Spending much time in prayer, I had promised God I would not compromise my priesthood nor would I be compromised as a priest.

On July 24, 1965, the church was overflowing with people, including my whole family, except my brother Chacour, who had died in 1961 while I was in Paris. Many relatives and friends attended, including Father Longère and forty others who had come all the way from France.

My two priest godfathers stood on either side of me, their hands on my shoulders, and loudly proclaimed, "The servant of God, Elias, is called to be priest, and he implores his Excellency, the archbishop of Galilee, to give him the sacrament of priesthood."

Then they led me to the altar, where I kissed the four corners three times each to symbolize my adherence to the gospel of Jesus Christ. I kneeled in front of the altar, my forehead resting against the cool stone. I could feel my pulse beating rapidly. Then the bishop laid his hand on my head. It was so heavy, but so loving.

"The power of the Holy Spirit that forgives every sin and fulfills every weakness will fulfill the servant of God, Elias, to become the priest of the high God and to serve the church on the altars of Galilee," intoned the bishop. Then, standing to the side of the altar, the bishop dressed me in my priestly vestments. With each piece he proclaimed in Greek, "*Axios, axios, axios.* He is worthy, he is worthy, he is worthy," and the people sang in reply, "He is worthy, he is worthy," in both Greek and Arabic.

I again paced in the churchyard. *Am I really worthy? Here I am suffering in Ibillin, wondering if I belong here, feeling utterly lost and sorry for myself. Is that being worthy of my calling? Lately I've begun to understand the pain the former priest must have felt. How many other priests are suffering just like me? Is worthiness somehow connected with suffering? Is that what it means to be a priest?*

God, I've been in Ibillin a month. Do you want me to stay and kill myself in the process? Do you want me to go to the bishop and ask for another parish? I was silent, staring into the darkness, exhausted from the emotional outpouring. *Or, do you have a special ministry for me here in this village? How can I be worthy of the gift you have given me?*

After a long while I wrapped myself in a blanket and lay down on my mat. Floating, drifting, I was a child in Biram once again, sleeping side by side with my brothers and sister on the main floor of the house with our parents on either end, keeping us covered with blankets.

Mother taught us Jesus' parable about a man who was sleeping with his wife and children in just this way. A friend in the village came at midnight, requesting bread for a guest. "No, don't bother me," the man said. "The door is shut and my children are with me in bed. I cannot get up and give you anything." He knew that the whole family would be aroused if one person got up. But because the one knocking on the door was persistent, the man finally gave him bread. Mother said, "Children, if you need something, tell your heavenly Father all about it. Don't be afraid and don't give up. Don't we need to fight with God sometimes to tell him we are so bothered by what's going on, that the storm is so big, and that God must do something? And, children, sometimes you might be angry with God. That does not mean you do not love God and that God does not love you. You are most angry with the one you love the most. So tell God just what you are feeling and what you need. Do not be afraid. Then trust the Lord and follow God's holy will."

Physical pain and hunger awakened me. *What can I do in this place, Lord? How do I reach my Melkite community?* What would happen, I wondered, if I started populating my loneliness with people, if I opened my own life, my own heart, mind, and eyes to others? What if I started knocking on *their* doors, visiting their homes, offering everything I have to give—myself and the boundless love of God? Drowsily I stared out the doorway into the moonlit churchyard. *Someday before the cold weather sets in I will make a door,* I promised myself, *a door I can close.*

Suddenly I sat up on the mat, wide awake. An open door! *Two* open doors! *It's perfect! This house will become an open house! I will invite everyone I visit. With God's help I will replace the loneliness with a lack of privacy, the noncommunication with talk and laughter, the fear and suspicion with hope and love. Every moment there should be people here to do something, to live, talk, and build something!*

Tomorrow I will start visiting, I vowed, as I lay down once again, smiling at the open doorway, which now represented such promise.

Chapter 3

The Tree Must Live!

"What is this?" the Responsible demanded, pointing at a healthy, sturdy plant growing at the edge of the churchyard. He and two other men were inspecting the church property, and I was accompanying them.

"That is a grapevine tree, my friend."

The Responsible narrowed his eyes. "I can see that it's a vine tree, Abuna. Do you think I'm stupid? I want to know where it came from and why it is here."

I took a wider stance and folded my arms across my chest. The moment of truth had come. "That vine tree is Habib's beautiful gift to me."

"What? You let that outsider, that communist, that deserter set foot on this property? You let him plant a vine tree here? How could you do such an idiotic thing?" the irate man sputtered.

"Habib just wanted to give me a gift. It's lovely, don't you think?"

"No, it's terrible!" the Responsible shouted. "He can't be allowed on this property. He went over to the Greek Orthodox church, and he's a traitor. First he'll claim the fruits and then he'll claim our church land. He's a damned communist and has been excommunicated by the bishop."

"Come on, my dear Responsible, Habib will not claim the fruits or the church land. He just wants me to have the grapes as a sign of friendship."

"You don't know Habib. I insist that you uproot this tree immediately." When the Responsible glared at the other men, they nodded.

I could see this man was determined to destroy the tree through his own blindness, bitterness, and anger, and thus kill every hope for any kind of reconciliation with Habib, but I was just as determined to have Habib as my friend. He was our next-door neighbor to the north of the church, and I had found him to be a gentle, kind, God-loving man.

"No, sir, I will not destroy the vine tree," I said. "It will stay."

"Abuna, you must uproot this vine tree or you will be kicked out of the village! Do you hear me?"

We stood staring at each other as he waited for my answer. What could I say to this poor, stubborn man? What could I do to convince him to let the vine tree live, to accept Habib's gift? How could the situation be transformed to one of peace and reconciliation?

Months before this confrontation, I had awakened early the morning after the decision to open my life to the people of Ibillin. I had begun visiting at nine o'clock, and by five that afternoon I was leaving the eighth home.

"Please," I said to Um Khalil (mother of Khalil, her oldest son), "tell Abu Khalil to come visit me at the parish house. And I would love to have you and the children visit me, too. Remember, when you see a light in the window, when you see I am at home, it means I am waiting for you all."

I waved and started walking up the dusty, stony street toward the parish house. My stomach was protesting the flood of coffee I had consumed, but my heart was light. I had done it! I had just started knocking on doors in the village and introducing myself. Not one door had slammed in my face. Because the men were at work, I had visited mostly women and children. I had answered the shy questions they asked, telling them about my Champion and myself, inviting them and their husbands to visit the church and me. Only time would tell if they accepted the invitations, but I had awakened that morning determined to have people in my two rooms. I wasn't going to tolerate my isolation and loneliness anymore.

19

The side benefit was that the women had given me not only coffee but also bread, hummus, olives, fruit, and sweets. I even had some bread and fruit for an evening meal.

Young Khalil and his friends were following me along the street. *Great!* I thought, smiling to myself. *Let me get the attention of the children and I'll soon have the attention of their parents.* "Come and visit me at the parish house and I'll tell you a story," I called to them. They ran away laughing, but I knew they'd be back someday with their friends.

My room felt alive. I could hear the voices of Um Issa, Um Said, Um Khalil, and all the children. *This is great,* I thought. *I want to know every family, every person who lives in Ibillin, regardless of their religion. I want to know this village inside and out, and I want the people to know me, to know that I care about them. When they feel free to visit with me, I will teach them the Bible stories, we will pray together, drink tea, and perhaps they'll begin to share themselves with me.* I felt affirmed in my decision to stay in Ibillin, to open the doors and my arms wide to these people. I didn't sleep much that night, thanks to all the coffee, but it didn't matter. I was busy making plans for my priesthood in Ibillin.

As the Responsible frequently reminded me, he was in charge of the church. This man had made of his position something much more than an overseer of property. He had appointed himself as overseer of the Melkite people, indeed, as the Omnipotent of Ibillin. In that role he could say whatever he chose and make judgments on anyone. The Melkite community was afraid of him and obeyed his commands, because he had proven in the past he had the power to punish and isolate people and even to persuade the bishop to anathematize them.

The Responsible soon heard about my daily round of visits. "I won't tolerate your visits to anyone except our Melkite community. Your time and attention belong to us, not to Muslims, not to the Orthodox, not to communists, not to outsiders. You work for us, understand? And all we want from you is to lead the liturgy, to pray and to baptize, marry and bury us. So do your work and everything will be fine." The Responsible considered me, the priest, to be part of the property of the church. I was to do his bidding and obey his commands, just as the other Melkites did.

Soon the Responsible began sending me written instructions with his youngest son at 7:30 each morning. The notes told me what I should and should not do that day, who I should and should not visit. He divided the villagers into two groups: acceptable and unacceptable. The list of "unacceptables" was very long indeed and included the Orthodox Christians, the Muslims, the communists, those who didn't like the church, and those who were "bad boys." I realized it was actually the Responsible who hated the church and that he caused others to hate the church as well. I found myself delighting in doing the contrary of the Responsible's wishes. He was teaching me how to disobey him.

Gradually people began visiting me. The men and women of the Melkite community stopped in to greet me and drink tea. The children ran in and out, sometimes stopping to hear a Bible story or two. Orthodox Christians visited, curious about this priest who seemed interested in them as well as his own community. Gradually the Muslim men came to call, too.

People also began to bring gifts of food. Early one morning while I was celebrating the Divine Liturgy alone, a young boy named Zahran quietly entered the church. Zahran approached me as I prayed, deposited on the altar a big dish covered with a newspaper, and said, "Take this from my mother." He ran away so quickly I barely saw who the child was. Carefully lifting the paper to peek into the dish, I found it filled with fresh, juicy figs. It was an excellent breakfast.

Late one evening I was working at my desk, reading and studying by the light of a petrol lamp. The night was quiet except for the occasional bray of a donkey or screech of a cat, but gradually I became aware of rustling noises accompanied by muffled voices outside my windows.

"Who is there?" I called, stepping out into the dark churchyard. "What do you want?" For a moment it was quiet and I was gripped with anxiety. Then two old men, Abu Karam and Abu Yacub, emerged from the shadows.

"What are you doing here, old men?" I said, laughing with relief. "Why don't you come in?"

"We don't want to come in," Abu Yacub said, patting my shoulder. "You've had enough people the whole day. We know that you are working."

"Then why are you going around and around the house?"

"Why, we're watching over you, Abuna," Abu Karam explained, "and we're praying for you so you'll know what to do and what to say. We know you are reading and writing things for us. By watching over you, we feel close to you, and you can know there's a presence right here with you." Then they melted back into the shadows and resumed their watching and praying.

The Responsible was furious about all my visitors. He was losing control of the people and the situation. Undoubtedly he knew he had no control over the new priest.

As I visited the homes, went into the business establishments, chatted with people in the street, and walked out in the village fields to greet the men at work, I was learning much about Ibillin. Freed from the fear of the Responsible, the people began to talk to me, and I heard about the great problems and divisions within the social, religious, and political fabric of the village. The seemingly tranquil village was teeming with anger, pain, and bitterness, and I discovered feuds that had gone on for years, even generations. I learned about the division between the Greek Orthodox people and the Melkites, between Christians and Muslims. I was told about the communists in the village and soon realized they were the people who protested social injustices such as land confiscation by the Israeli government and who tried to do something to help. The ones who called themselves communists were both Muslim and Christian. I found that many of the Christians who were communists were very strong believers in the teachings of Christ and tried to put them into action.

In Ibillin there was a general store called "the communist store." It belonged to the local communist party. I passed that establishment frequently, and each time I waved at the men standing by the doorway. They suspended their conversation to watch me, but none waved a greeting in return. Being the Melkite priest, I was suspect because of their previous experiences. Nevertheless, I continued waving to those people every time I passed the store.

"I heard you are going to visit your neighbor Habib," the Responsible wrote one morning. "Don't forget that Habib is an outsider, a communist. He was a Greek Catholic and he changed to become Greek Orthodox. You are not to visit the cursed, damned house of that excommunicated communist."

It was true. I was planning to visit Habib in his home very soon. As usual, the Responsible's opposition made me want to do the forbidden thing all the more. *Today,* I thought, *today I will visit Habib.*

At three o'clock that afternoon the Responsible paid his daily call. As we visited in the churchyard, I saw Habib going up the stairs of his house, returning from work. Excusing myself, I left the Responsible and quickly went to Habib's house, walking up the outside stairs to the first landing.

I looked down into the churchyard and called to the Responsible, "I know what you think of this visit. I read your instructions, but I also read the gospel and I know the people in this family are children of God. Christ would not have waited this long to visit with them. My visit won't be lengthy, my dear Responsible, and you can wait for me if you wish. Otherwise, I will see you tomorrow."

The Responsible stared at me, his mouth open. Without waiting for a reply, I turned and saw Habib smiling a welcome in the doorway.

"Welcome to my home, Abuna," this bad communist, this rejected Christian, said, shaking my hand and ushering me into his house.

Habib's wife, Um Fat'hee, served us fruit, sweets, and coffee as we visited. I was fascinated by this man who had been so vilified by the Responsible. What sort of person was he? Habib seemed just as curious about me, the priest who was visiting everyone in the village and who had incurred the wrath of the Responsible.

"Tell me, Habib," I said, peeling a juicy orange, "why did you leave the Melkite community back in the early 1950s?"

"First let me say, Abuna, that it was not my desire to leave. I was born in that community, and I loved it. I still do. But I also love the land here in Galilee, the land of our ancestors. My father and my father's father's father have lived on this particular land of Ibillin and grown their olives and figs, their tomatoes and cucumbers."

I nodded, remembering Biram and how my father had described his love for the land and his trees.

"The Israeli government began confiscating our land in the late 1940s, and it continued into the fifties and sixties. We here in Ibillin have lost thousands of *dunums* [four dunums equal one acre], land that has simply been taken by the Israeli government.[1]

"Some of us in the village, particularly those calling ourselves communists today, loudly protested the confiscation of our land," Habib said, smiling wryly, "and we got in lots and lots of trouble."

"What sort of trouble?"

"The trouble came from the Israeli government, the police, and also from the bishop and many members of the Melkite community. We were condemned by those people, and many of us were arrested. More land was taken. And, Abuna, whether you want to believe it or not, the Melkite bishop was sympathetic not to us who were losing the land but to the Israeli government. He was aligned with them against us, his own people."

I had heard this story before from other villagers. *How could the bishop have deserted his people when they needed him so much?* I wondered. *How could he align himself with the oppressor?*

"The situation got so bad here in the village that many of us who were protesting were isolated from the Melkite community by the bishop and by people like the Responsible. 'Unless you keep silent,' the bishop told us, 'you are Christians no more.' One day one of the protesters died, and the bishop refused to let his funeral take place in the church. Later someone wanted to get married, and the bishop said he couldn't be married in the church because he had protested. Finally we asked the Greek Orthodox priest, Abuna Ibrahim, if we could pray with his community of Christians, and he welcomed us. About two hundred Melkites became Orthodox. It was a terribly painful experience. Even now, I know we are not forgiven by our Melkite relatives and friends." He sadly shook his head.

The next week Habib came to visit me. "Abuna," he said, "I think you are a good man and I want to give you a present." In his hands he had a small grapevine tree and a young lemon tree. Together we planted them in the churchyard. The vine tree was planted right near Habib's house.

"Thank you very much, my friend," I said. "I will care for it and speak to it often about its significance. Surely the vine tree will grow and bear much fruit."

"Well?" the Responsible insisted. "Are you going to uproot this despicable vine tree? Or am I going to do it for you?"

"Would you bring me a bucket of water?" I asked the Responsible. While it was being fetched, I walked over to the lovely vine tree. What a shame to destroy the tree and the trust and friendship I enjoyed with Habib.

"Now you're being sensible, Abuna," the Responsible said when I took the bucket. "The water will loosen the soil, and the tree will come out."

I poured the water all over the vine tree, dousing its branches, leaves, and trunk. Then I made the sign of the cross with my right hand over the dripping plant and said, "Oh, vine tree, I baptize you Christian in the name of the Father, the Son, and the Holy Spirit. The one who uproots you will be uprooted. The one who waters you will be watered by God's grace."

I threw the bucket aside as I turned to speak to the startled Responsible. "My dear sir, uproot the tree now if you can. But you can't. It will grow and become very, very big."

I left the Responsible and his two friends staring at the newly baptized tree. I knew they would not dare touch it now. I also knew, however, that although the vine tree would grow and flourish, there was much to be done to allow the villagers the same opportunity.

Chapter 4

Palm Sunday Prisoners

"How are you, Faraj?" I cried. "I have missed you so much! Are you enjoying your ministry in Rama?" I had so many questions to ask my old friend Faraj that the poor man could barely say a word. Bishop Hakim had called a special meeting in Nazareth for all the priests of the diocese. It was the first time Faraj and I had seen each other since our ordination.

"It's wonderful and things are going well. Oh, I have missed you, too, Elias! Tell me all about yourself and about Ibillin!"

These words were so precious, so beautiful to me. Another priest had finally asked about my parish and my circumstances there. I opened my mouth to tell my dear friend about the hardships and pain I had endured and how I felt abandoned in this small village, things I had wanted so desperately to share with the bishop and other priests. But the words that came out surprised even me.

"Ibillin is a wonderful place, Faraj. The people have been very good to me. And I have learned so much from them. There's Habib, my next-door neighbor who has become my friend. And there's the Responsible—well, what can I say? He's such a challenge to me and my ministry. And the children, the children, Faraj! They come to my room, and I tell them stories from the Bible, just like my mother used to tell me."

Faraj listened and nodded. His smile was warm, his eyes very bright and caring. It was like being back in Paris again, sharing our innermost thoughts.

"At the same time, Faraj, there are many problems in the village. People in some families haven't spoken to each other in

26

years because of divisive feuds. Christians and Muslims, Orthodox and Melkites often hate each other. People with different political ideas are bitterly fighting.

"Once I tried to give a lecture on ecumenism, which was a complete failure. The only good result was the note a Melkite man named Ruhe left on a nail in my doorway:

> You are coming to preach ecumenism? This is useless. We don't want it. Begin first to reconcile brothers, sisters, families together. This is the ecumenism we need. We don't want to be lost in vague ideas.

The words stung, Faraj, because I knew they were absolutely true."

"And have you found ways to effect reconciliation, Elias?"

"Not yet. I am listening to the multitude of problems, to the great pain the people are sharing with me. I am watching the relationships and learning as much as possible. For instance, there's Um Daoud, who hasn't spoken to her sister for twenty years. And there's a villager, Abu Muhib, who is an Israeli policeman, a tough and difficult man. He is hated and feared by almost everyone, including members of his own family. I greet him in the street and am instantly criticized by the villagers. The divisions are very deep in Ibillin. I pray every day that God will give me the wisdom and courage to address them effectively."

Faraj frowned a little, regarding me closely. "You look thinner to me, Elias. Are you eating enough? And sleeping well?"

"Oh, yes," I said, waving his concern aside. "Things were a little rough at the beginning, but the people have been very generous with their food. I cannot complain on that count at all." I decided not to mention that I was still sleeping in the backseat of my car when I got tired of the cement floor. "Everything is going very well. Now, tell me about your situation in Rama."

As I listened to Faraj describe his ministry in Rama, his hometown, I realized his experience had been very different from mine. I soon learned he was sleeping in a bed and had plenty to eat. I was grateful because I loved Faraj very much and wouldn't have wanted him to have to cope with the problems I continued to face in Ibillin.

Yes, I decided, I was proud of my parish, and the words that had so quickly leaped out of my mouth in praise of Ibillin and its people were exactly what I wanted the world to know. I wanted to build up my people and their shattered dignity, focus on the good things that were happening, and throw out a challenge to others to also build up things in their ministries. At the same time I wanted to help my people be reconciled with each other, freeing them from their prisons of pain, hatred, and bitterness.

Ibillin has a verifiable history of continuous Christian population and presence from about the first or second century A.D. In the 1980s a Christian cemetery from the second century was discovered containing pottery and glass marked with ancient Christian symbols such as the fish, the lamb, and bread. Indeed, the village of Ibillin was the see of the archbishop of Zebulon already in the fourth and fifth centuries. One of the bishops present at the Council of Nicea in A.D. 325 was Bishop Nisifos from Ibillin.[1]

Ibillin became a headquarters for the Crusader leader the French Count of Abelin in the thirteenth century. The villagers discovered the walls of the Crusader city of Ibillin in the 1970s while building the community center.

The present Melkite church, dating from the seventeenth century, was built on the ruins of an ancient Byzantine church from the fourth century and a Crusader church from the eleventh and twelfth centuries. In 1920 a new altar area and narthex were added to the main bulk of the seventeenth-century church. The well and cistern underneath the sanctuary, originally intended to supply baptismal water, were more recently closed and filled, but the humidity from the clay cementing inside the walls of the church continues to cause mildew, peeling paint, and decomposition problems.

Whenever I say the liturgy in this church, I have a strong sense of continuity with Galilean Christian brothers and sisters over the centuries, disciples of Jesus of Nazareth, a town only about thirty kilometers away.

Nevertheless, I awakened very early on Palm Sunday 1966 feeling anxious and distressed. The prospect of singing the liturgy and celebrating the Eucharist on this feast day seemed like a huge burden as I contemplated the severe problems in my community.

O God, I know that you are Lord and only through your will and your power can these problems of hatred be overcome. So, God, what do I do now? Do I just leave the people to their own devices? Do I continue to challenge them to a life of love and compassion? Do I scold and lecture them? Do I just try to live my own life as an example of your loving care? What can I possibly say this Palm Sunday morning that I haven't said before? O God, help me. And help these people.

The Responsible rang the bell at 9:30 a.m., and the people began coming into the church. As I finished putting on my ornamental vestment, an elegant white satin robe with red decorative stitching, I could see that many more people than usual were seated on the benches. A few minutes later the Responsible came into the altar area appearing flushed and excited.

"Abuna, there is such a crowd of people that we have run out of room. There must be more than 250 people in the church, and others are standing outside, wanting to come in. What will we do?"

A glance through the archway confirmed the Responsible's words. "Well, bring them right in here," I said, pointing to the altar area.

Ordinarily the Responsible probably would not have agreed to such an unusual solution, but because of the tremendous crush of people he quickly turned and began ushering them through the side archway. The people were amazed to find themselves behind the iconostasis with the priest. They stood close to the wall, giving me and the altar boys just enough room to celebrate the liturgy.

Everything went smoothly through the Liturgy of St. John Chrysostom. Abu Jirius and a few others sang the responses, and the two young altar boys did everything I had taught them to do. A sizable number of people came to receive Holy Communion, too.

Despite the crowd of people, despite the increase in communicants, however, I was continuing to feel uneasy and burdened. I could see so many people who were at odds with each other. Abu Muhib had come to church this Palm Sunday dressed in his Israeli police uniform. Ordinarily no one except his wife and children would have sat near him, but today with such a crowd he was jammed in like the rest. Um Daoud was there with her family, but her sister and her family were on the other side of the church. The Responsible was standing toward the back of the church, his arms folded on his chest, surveying what he perceived as his kingdom. And there was Ruhe, whose written message was burned in my brain: "Begin first to reconcile brothers and sisters and families, Abuna." But every time I turned around to bless the congregation, to give them Christ's peace, I was reminded all over again that there was in reality no peace among these people. Such peace had always been refused.

As the liturgy ended, I made my decision. Before anyone could move, I hurried down the center aisle, startling the worshipers. Usually a priest wearing his ornaments remains behind the iconostasis while the people file out. But here I was striding among them, a determined look on my face, my long sleeves looking like wings as they filled with the breeze I was creating. I walked directly to the two doors on either side of the main part of the church, locking both doors while the people watched me, silently frozen in place.

I took the big, old key, marched back up the aisle, stepped into the main archway, and turned around to face the people. Loudly and firmly, I said, "I want you to know how beloved you all are to me and how saddened I am to find you hating and decrying each other. I have tried so often in the six months I have been here to help you reconcile with each other, but I have been unable to do so. I have wondered if all the villages have the problems you have here, and I tell you the truth when I say that I have looked about in Galilee and have found that you are alone in such bitterness and hatred. You are very, very complicated people here in Ibillin." It was deathly silent in the church. I could see no movement among the people.

"This morning while I celebrated the liturgy, I found someone who is able to help you. In fact, he is the only one who can work the miracle of reconciliation in this village. This person who can reconcile you is Jesus Christ, and he is here with us. We are gathered in his name, this man who rode in triumph into Jerusalem with hosannas from the people ringing in his ears.

"So on Christ's behalf, I say this to you: The doors of the church are locked. Either you kill each other right here in your hatred and then I will celebrate your funerals gratis, or you use this opportunity to be reconciled together before I open the doors of the church. If that reconciliation happens, Christ will truly become your Lord, and I will know I am becoming your pastor and your priest. That decision is now yours."

The people were starting to look around at each other. A few men seemed to want to leave but I put up my hand and stopped them.

"No, don't try to get out. The doors are locked. And the key is in my hand. You can take this key only if you kill me. The only other way you will get out of here is to make peace among yourselves by being reconciled to those whom you have hurt and who have hurt you."

I stood in the archway with my hands folded in front of me, looking out over the captive congregation. No one said a word. They looked at me, they looked at each other, they looked at the peeling paint on the dome and arches, they looked at the floor. The silence continued.

I steadfastly stared at the people. There they were, almost my entire Melkite community, gathered for the festive day of Palm Sunday. Now they had been taken captive by a crazy priest.

Cars passed on the road alongside the church. People walking by outside called to one another. A donkey brayed, and children laughed. A late rooster crowed his greeting to the world. And the Melkites sat in silence, locked inside their church.

A full ten minutes passed. I could feel the perspiration running down my back, a huge knot of fear clutching my stomach. *O God, what have I done? Is this yet another failure?* Knowing I could do nothing but continue on the path I had chosen, I stood in front of my congregation, now with my arms folded across my chest. My parents, brothers, and sister could have told these people how stubborn Elias could be.

Then I detected a slight movement among the people. To my utter amazement I saw Abu Muhib slowly stand up, his police uniform instantly identifying him to every eye in the church. He stretched out his arms and looked about him, and then looked toward me. "Abuna, I ask forgiveness of everybody here and I forgive everybody. And I ask God to forgive me my sins."

I stepped down to the church floor and reached out my arms toward the lone figure standing in the congregation. "Fine," I cried to him, "this is excellent! Come here, come here, Abu Muhib! Let me hug you!"

The policeman struggled to get out of his row and then came striding down the aisle toward me, tears running down his face, his arms stretched out. We hugged each other at the front of the church, dampening each other's faces with our tears. Then, still holding Abu Muhib's arm, I shouted to the people, "Why don't we hug each other now? I will hug everybody, and everybody will hug each other, all right?"

Everyone stood up and began coming forward. They hugged me in my ornamental vestments. They hugged Abu Muhib and stood in line to hug everyone else who came along behind them. Tears and laughter mingled as people who had said such ugly words to each other or who had not spoken to each other in many years now were sharing Christ's love and peace.

After everyone had been hugged, I shouted, "Don't listen to gossipers and to people who are only interested in seeing you dispersed, divided from each other again. Now you are one community.

"Brothers and sisters, this is not Palm Sunday any longer. This is our resurrection! We are a community that has risen from the dead, and we have new life. I propose that we don't wait until next Sunday, until Easter, to celebrate the resurrection. I will unlock the doors and then let us go from home to home all over the village and sing the resurrection hymn to everyone!"

The people even then began to sing the resurrection hymn as they streamed out the open church doors:

Christ is risen from the dead!
By his death he has trampled upon death
And has given life to those
Who are in the tomb!

All afternoon I could hear singing, ululations, happy voices, and laughter. I knew this was a whole new life for Ibillin. Like a mother who had given birth to a beautiful baby after hours of hard labor, I now forgot the pain and the hardship. I only saw this vision of my parish reconciling together.

I grew up knowing that forgiveness brings healing and peace. My parents went to the church in Biram every Saturday evening to attend vespers, a service of evening prayer that ended with the confession of sins. Then Mother and Father would come back home, and before we ate, they would ask for our forgiveness, saying, "Children, we love you. We might have hurt you in some way this week; if so, we ask your forgiveness. If we have failed you in any way, please forgive us." That is the most beautiful image I remember of my family.

Late on Palm Sunday afternoon I removed the locks from the church doors and threw them away, along with the key. Never again would these doors be locked as long as I was priest in Ibillin. The unlocked church doors would be a symbol of our new trust and openness.

Now the doors are open on both the church and the parish house, I thought, as I swept away the remains of the destroyed locks. I had addressed my community and led them to a time of reconciliation. I had encouraged them to reach out to everyone in the village with their forgiveness and love. Now what? How could we build on the foundation established today?

Chapter 5

A New Jeremiah Speaks

"Good morning, Abuna Ibrahim," I called, seeing the Greek Orthodox priest sitting under a carob tree in his large, pleasant yard. "I have come to visit you."

The enmity that existed between the Melkites and the Orthodox in this village needed to be addressed, I decided the week after Palm Sunday. The first step toward justice, peace, and reconciliation was up to me, the new priest in town, who wasn't burdened with the heavy load of history.

"Good morning, Abuna Elias," the eighty-six-year-old man said, rising slowly to greet me and shake my hand. "You are most welcome here."

Our conversation was delightful, and I soon discovered I had a friend and confidant in the wise, elderly Orthodox priest of Ibillin.

"Abuna Elias," he asked, smiling broadly, "did you actually lock the Melkites in the church until they reconciled with each other?"

"Yes, Abuna Ibrahim, I did."

"O my Lord, I wish I could have been there to see that!" The old priest roared in delight, and I soon joined him. Passersby saw two abunas laughing and giggling like children, slapping their knees and each other's shoulders, wiping away tears.

After enjoying tea and fruit, I spoke of the troubles between the Melkites and Orthodox. Abuna Ibrahim sighed and shook his head.

"I was here in Ibillin in 1948 when the Jewish Zionist soldiers were going from village to village. We were frightened, having heard the stories of tragedies and even massacre, such as the killing of 250 Palestinians in Deir Yassin near Jerusalem.[1] Many people fled to what they thought were safer places, temporarily leaving their homes. Others of us stayed, believing we could protect our property and our families. I was young then, Abuna Elias, not quite seventy years old.

"Many Palestinian refugees came flooding into Ibillin. Some lived in the empty houses, others in tents in the fields, and others just lived under the trees. Daily the Zionist soldiers threatened us with the loss of our property and even of our lives. Many priests and bishops fled, leaving their people to fend for themselves. I could not do that, no matter what happened to me personally. I am a Palestinian, not a foreigner." He sighed deeply and scrutinized my face with his dark, alert eyes.

"Not only the priests and bishops left, but also most of our civic leadership. The Palestinian social and political structure here in Galilee was destroyed, and each village had to take care of itself. Needless to say, no help came from the Israeli government. The Arab Palestinian people inside the new state were unwanted, seen as a security threat, owning land that was desired by Israel.

"Before long the Israeli government was confiscating our farming land. Thousands of dunums were claimed by the government, just swallowed up. Once it was claimed, we could not even set foot on it. The land was simply declared necessary for military purposes or declared to be state land, and that was that.[2]

"The combination of pressure and injustice from the Israeli government and the collapse of the Palestinian social structure created tremendous problems here in the village and all over Galilee. The people were fighting among themselves about how to handle the problems, just when they needed to be working together. Great divisions occurred in Ibillin. Some people wanted to fight the land confiscation, others just wanted to get along with the Israeli government, and most were very confused.

"The ones who protested were Orthodox, Melkite, and Muslim, and they all suffered greatly for expressing their views. These God-fearing people were punished by the Israeli government and also by some of their fellow Palestinians, but they chose to take the risk of speaking out rather than simply accepting injustice."

I nodded. "So they became outcasts among their own people, even in the eyes of the church."

"Exactly. Exactly so," Abuna Ibrahim answered, punctuating his words with his walking stick. "And I must confess to you that I was much in sympathy with these protesters. I encouraged them and prayed with them."

"I would have done the same thing," I assured the old priest.

"Some of the protesters in the Melkite community came to me and poured out their troubles. They had been excommunicated by the bishop and could not be baptized, married, or buried in the church. They did not want to be Orthodox, but they wanted and needed to be in communion with the church.

"Well, I ask you, Abuna Elias," the old priest said, leaning forward in his chair, challenging me with his eyes and words, "how could I deny God's grace in the sacraments to these people? I initially thought twenty or thirty people might come to our church, but the count eventually reached nearly two hundred. I know I've been hated by the Melkites ever since."

Abuna Ibrahim held out his hand to me, and I took it. When he spoke again, his voice was gravelly and cracked with emotion. "Abuna Elias, I confess to you that I have sinned. I have not been loving and kind to those who hated me. I ask you to forgive me. I do not want to live with such disunity and enmity any longer." Penitential tears now flowed.

I felt humble in the presence of this holy man, and my own tears spilled over. "Abuna Ibrahim, I do forgive you in the name of God the Father, the Son, and the Holy Spirit. And I ask you to forgive me for my hasty judgments and my selfish thoughts."

"I forgive you, my son," Abuna Ibrahim whispered, "and you are forgiven by the Lord Jesus Christ."

On my way home from Abuna Ibrahim's house, I passed the communist store.

"*Salaam alekhum*, peace be to you," I called out to the men, waving at them the way I always did. "It's a beautiful day, don't you agree?"

As usual the men silently watched me approach, but this time, before I could pass by, all of them smiled and waved at me. From that day onward, whenever I passed the communist store, the men always raised their hands in greeting before I could wave at them. They finally knew that this priest respected and loved them. The Palm Sunday attitude was proving to be infectious.

"Abuna, we want you to baptize little Ibrahim, my grandson." The old woman and her daughter-in-law, the child's mother, had lingered to speak with me privately after the liturgy.

"Fine. I'd be most delighted to baptize him." This would be the first baptism I had performed as a priest.

The Byzantine ritual of baptism requires nearly three-quarters of an hour. The child is momentarily immersed in the baptistry after having been anointed with the blessed oil. Then chrismation occurs, another anointing with oil that bestows the gift of the Holy Spirit. After a child has been baptized, he or she may receive Holy Communion each Sunday.

When I took naked, squirming, two-month-old Ibrahim in my hands, carefully holding him as a mother would hold her baby, I was very moved. I was the instrument by which this tiny, squealing baby was being born in Christ.

A few weeks later I visited Bishop Hakim in Haifa. "Bishop, I was privileged to baptize a little baby boy!"

"How much money did you take for the baptism?"

"I did not take any money, Bishop," I stammered, caught off guard. "They gave me a gift of two pounds [about one U.S. dollar]."

The bishop was incensed. "Two pounds? And you accepted that? Abuna Elias, I forbid you to accept any less than five pounds for a baptism. Otherwise, you are setting a bad example by encouraging the people to give small amounts. If other priests, your colleagues, come to do a baptism and receive less than five pounds, they will be very upset."

Gone was the rush of joy I had wanted to share with my bishop. Taking its place I could feel angry determination and stubbornness.

"Bishop Hakim, I promise you in the presence of God that as long as God gives me the privilege to work as a priest, I will never, ever accept any money at all from anybody for any religious service." Shaking with fury, I stalked out of the bishop's office.

How incredible! How could my bishop focus on the money and not on the miracle of baptism itself? Faraj and I had often spoken about the danger of a priest exploiting his people, but I had never dreamed I would see it in my own bishop.

That evening at the altar in the church, I repeated my vow. When my anger subsided, I begged God to give me the strength not to succumb to the temptation of money and wealth, thereby harming my people. Finally I was able to pray for my poor bishop, whom I loved so dearly.

In July 1966 Faraj and I met again at the annual priests' retreat in Nazareth. Our initial enchantment with the idea of being priests had blended into the reality of daily tasks and responsibilities. Later I would recall that Faraj seemed tired and did not walk as rapidly as he had in Paris. At the time I dismissed it as fatigue due to the summer heat.

On the last morning of the retreat Bishop Hakim seated Faraj and me on his right and left hands for the farewell breakfast. It was traditional for each priest to stand and say a few words to the bishop. I soon understood what was happening. The bishop was receiving fine flattery from his priests.

"Bishop Hakim, you are a prince of the church. You are recognized as such by all of us and also by the patriarch," one priest exclaimed.

"Hear, hear," the priests rejoined.

An elderly priest then stood to say, "My bishop, it is not too much to state that you are, without a doubt, the most brilliant Arab personality in Israel today. Am I right?" he asked the other priests.

"Oh, yes," they cried, "you are absolutely right!"

Yet another priest proclaimed, "Bishop Hakim, you are the most generous benefactor this diocese has ever known. Our people owe you so much for the churches and schools you have built, as well as for private gifts."

"Well, my sons," the bishop addressed Faraj and me when the applause subsided, "what do you have to say to us? Abuna Faraj? Will you speak?" Faraj suddenly turned very shy and shook his head, smiling.

"Well, then, Abuna Elias, it is up to you to speak," the bishop said, turning to me. I, too, shook my head. The smile on the bishop's face was beginning to look a little strained. "Now, now, I *must* hear something from these two young priests whom I ordained just a year ago." Still Faraj and I resisted the invitation, feeling the eyes of the priests boring into us.

"Abuna Faraj, Abuna Elias, truly I insist that one of you must speak." The bishop's voice now had an authoritarian edge to it that could not be ignored. Faraj, being a very stubborn boy, outlasted me.

I finally stood up, much to the relief of everyone else in the room. I adjusted my gray cassock and smoothed my beard, turning to face Bishop Hakim, who was now beaming in anticipation of my words. "Well, my dear, beloved bishop, you have heard all these other priests praise you, but when you ask me to speak, I hesitate because I am like Jeremiah. You remember that when Jeremiah was asked to speak, he said to God, 'Oh please, I am but a little boy who babbles. I cannot speak well.' And God said to Jeremiah, 'Do not say, "I am a child." I am putting my words into your mouth. Look, today I am setting you . . . to tear up and to knock down, to destroy and to overthrow, to build and to plant.'"

The room had become very quiet. Even the bishop had stopped smiling and was concentrating on my words.

I swallowed hard. Once again I was speaking dangerous, challenging words. I had no option but to plow forward. "It is with the spirit that God gave to Jeremiah that I tell you, Bishop, I am not proud of you if you are a prince of the church. And if you are a highly ranked politician in this country and if you distribute much money, I am not proud of you."

The bishop stared at me without blinking. Faraj's face was tense, his jaw set.

"Rather, Bishop, I will be proud of you whenever I see you humbling yourself, washing and kissing the feet of your parishioners and your priests. It is then that I will see in you Jesus Christ, the Man from Galilee. It is then I will see not the prince, not the social leader, not the person grasping for money and for power, but the servant. Bishop, it is the Christlike servant that I am waiting to see more and more in you. Then I will open my mouth and be proud of you." I quickly sat down.

The bishop was silent for a long moment. Then he laid his big hands on the table in front of him, looked around at all of us with his penetrating eyes, and said, "Well, this Jeremiah is not worse than the first." And all the priests breathed again.

After the 1967 war I visited with a French priest at Ecole Biblique in East Jerusalem. He told me that Bishop Hakim had spent a whole week there in prayer after the conference in Nazareth. "Tell me, Abuna Elias," the French priest asked, "who was that priest that dared say to Bishop Hakim that he expected him to wash the feet of his people?"

I loved and respected my bishop more at that moment than I would have ever thought possible. His prayers in Jerusalem, his sharing what must have been a difficult and embarrassing incident in his life—all this was a sign to me of the true greatness and genuine humility of Bishop Hakim, a man of prayer.

"But, Abuna, if the man was paralyzed, how could he get inside the house to see Jesus?" Marwan asked. The other girls and boys looked at me with wide, expectant eyes. This was the fourth week I had invited the children to hear a Bible story on Sunday afternoon. More than sixty boys and girls, two grandmothers, and a few teenage young women had gathered in the church.

"The man had good friends and relatives who helped him. Jesus was sitting inside a house and the owner, probably Peter, had seated him in the place of honor. You all know where that is in your houses, don't you?"

The children nodded their heads. Guests of honor were still seated with their backs to the inside wall, facing the outer door, just as they had been in Jesus' lifetime here in Galilee.

40

"The paralyzed man's friends saw how crowded the house was, so they carried him up to the flat roof and found an opening. . . ."

A child interrupted me. "Abuna, we have an opening in our roof, too. That's where we put the hay for the animals into the storage room in our house!"

"Yes, I know. When I was growing up, there was a storage room in my house, too, and there was an opening in the flat roof. That's exactly the place the man's friends found. And then they carefully lowered the paralyzed man down into the house until he was right near Jesus."

Feda could not contain her excitement. "And did Jesus make the man walk again, Abuna?"

"First Jesus said, 'My son, your sins are forgiven,' and then he said, 'Rise, take up your bed, and go home.' What do you think happened then, Feda?"

"The man walked home! He did! He did!" she shouted, and the other children cheered.

"Yes, the man was healed, and he walked home carrying his bed. Everyone was so happy, just as you are, and they glorified God, saying 'We've never seen anything like this!'

"Today I want you all to go home and tell your families about the strong trust those people had in God. That's the kind of faith and trust we all can have in our Friend and Champion Jesus Christ."

The future of our Melkite community in Ibillin rested on the tiny shoulders of these children. My task as their priest was to help them love the Lord Jesus Christ and to feel as comfortable in the church as they did in their own houses. Ministering to the children was beginning to be of vast importance to me. I found myself dreaming of all sorts of ways in which I could reach the boys and girls of Ibillin. My dreams were taking on dimensions that I knew I could not handle by myself. If even some of my hopes were fulfilled, I would need help to implement the reality.

Chapter 6

Where Is God?

"There are stories in the New Testament about people just like us who lived in villages in Galilee," I told the young women in the Wednesday Bible class. "Turn to the Gospel of Luke, chapter 15. Here we find three stories Jesus told about things that were lost."

The young women had been coming to the children's Bible story hours on Sunday afternoons, but I knew they needed more depth in the Scripture. For several months we had gathered weekly to read the New Testament together.

"The first story is about a lost sheep and how a shepherd searched for it. Have you ever searched and searched for something that was lost?"

Miriam raised her hand. "One time my family and I had to search for our cow. My brother Issa let her wander away. We looked everywhere for that cow, even up on Jabal el Ghoul, the Mount of the Ogre, but we couldn't find her. Late in the evening everyone in our family and many of our neighbors were still searching for that cow in the moonlight. Finally my father and my uncle Khalil heard the voice of the poor cow. She was caught in some high, prickly bushes on the other side of the fields."

"What happened when your father brought the cow back to the village?"

"Oh, there was a great celebration with food and dancing! It went on until early the next morning."

"Now why should there be such a celebration for the return of a lost cow? It's just an animal." I pretended to be ignorant.

"Oh, Abuna," Rawda protested, "we need our cows to plant the fields, plow the land, and help move big rocks. If we

42

didn't have our cows, we would not have much food to eat, trade, or sell."

"And what would have happened if the cow had been found with her leg trapped and broken between some rocks, for example?"

"The cow would have had to be slaughtered," Gislaine answered, "and her owner would have distributed the meat to all his friends and acquaintances."

"And those people would have given the man gifts of money for the meat to help him buy a new cow immediately," Miriam added. "The same thing would have happened if it had been a lamb or a sheep that was lost."

Together we read Jesus' story about the lost sheep, and my companions exclaimed over the similarities to their own experiences.

"Now notice that the next few verses tell about a woman who lost one silver coin and then swept her house until she found it."

"Abuna, once this happened in the church," Zada said. "Um Rami dropped her money for the offering, and we had to get a petrol lamp and search for the coins. We couldn't see them because the floor was so dark."

"That's right, Zada," I told the young woman, who taught at the village kindergarten. "In many homes and churches we have these dirt floors that are protected and sealed with the dark, oily residue from the olive presses. It was the same when Jesus lived in Nazareth so many years ago. Like us, the people lost things on the dark floors."

The responses from their own experiences pleased me. I wanted so much to help these young Palestinian women identify with Jesus Christ, this Man of Galilee, this Palestinian, who was their Savior and Friend. In fact, they also were revealing Christ to me.

"In the next verses we find the story of the loving father who welcomes back the prodigal boy that we know as the lost son.

"Tell me, who is Jesus talking about when he speaks of the shepherd, the woman with the broom, and the loving father?"

The young women pored over the passages. "It must be God, Abuna."

"Why do you say that?"

"Well," Rawda ventured, "it is God who loves us so much that he comes to find us when we are lost. I believe God is happy when he can bring us back where we belong."

"And how does God come to look for us, to find us?"

Answers were quickly given. "In the Bible, with all the stories. . . . Through the Divine Liturgy. . . . In Holy Communion. . . . When we are baptized."

"Yes, those are all ways in which God comes to us and helps us become like him. But there's another way you haven't mentioned yet."

Miriam spoke hesitantly. "Maybe these stories are a way of saying that God comes to us in Jesus Christ."

"Exactly, Miriam. Jesus lived here in Galilee as a human being just like us. Everyone can learn from him who God is and what God is like.

"Just as the sheep was precious to the shepherd and the coin was precious to the woman, each person is precious to God and of inestimable worth and value. God teaches us to love our fellow human beings not out of charity or pity, nor even to please God, but because every person is lovable and deserves to be loved. Why? Because every human being—every Christian, Muslim, Jew, Palestinian, American, or Russian—is in the image and likeness of God."

Each Friday I took my Bible study group somewhere in Galilee to visit the holy places about which they were learning. In 1966 and 1967 the Israeli government still insisted that Arab Palestinians living inside Israel must have permits to travel anywhere. Each week I applied to the military governor in Akko to obtain these permits. For most of the young women it was a rare opportunity to leave the village, get out of the depressing loneliness and isolation, and particularly to see the nearby places where Jesus had lived and worked. On past excursions we had visited the Mount of Beatitudes, the Sea of Galilee, and Mount Carmel.

On this particular Friday we drove to the top of Mount Tabor on the hairpin road lined with trees. Mount Tabor, often called the Mount of Transfiguration, is located at the north-eastern end of the plain of Jezreel, Megiddo, or Esdraelon. Only a few kilometers from Nazareth, Mount Tabor soars above the plain, appearing very majestic. Here Deborah and Barak gathered with the armies that defeated General Sisera. Early Christian tradition teaches it was to this mountain that Jesus took Peter, James, and John to be witnesses of his transfiguration. Mount Tabor was very familiar to me. Time and again I had walked from Nazareth to the top of this mountain, often with Faraj. On the way we collected flowers and ate many different herbs and seeds. We learned to live as a part of our beloved Galilee as did our Compatriot Jesus Christ.

At the top of the mountain our Bible study group first visited the Church of the Transfiguration and then started exploring the land. The view from this mountain, a cone-shaped block of limestone, is truly magnificent. To the northeast Mount Hermon can be seen, blanketed with snow. On the east are the Golan Heights, which look over the quiet Sea of Galilee and the Jordan depression along the Afro-Asian Great Rift Valley. To the south is the little village of Nain, where Jesus raised the widow's son from the dead, and beyond that the hills of Samaria. To the west stretches the green, fertile plain of Jezreel. All of this land Jesus traversed many times, alone and with his disciples.

Finally we settled down on a grassy area to eat our lunch. Gislaine, Zada, Rawda, and Miriam, along with the other young women, had packed bread, cheese, fruit, and delicious Arab sweets. We feasted on the food and the panorama in front of us. The centuries-old history of God and humanity was wide open to us.

"Jesus walked with Peter, James, and John up on this mountain, just as we drove here today," I said. "The disciples were tired after that long climb, and they went to sleep while Jesus was praying. As he prayed, his face began to shine, his clothes became dazzling white, and Moses and Elijah came to speak with him.

"Imagine how shocked Peter, James, and John must have been when they awakened and saw Jesus' glory. What a surprise to see Moses and Elijah! Peter wanted to build three little tents up here so everyone could stay forever, contemplating the transfigured Lord.

"A great cloud came and overshadowed them all," I told my companions, "and when the cloud was gone, Jesus was alone again, looking the way they had always known him.

"The true beauty of this transfiguration was that the disciples themselves were transfigured. Their eyes were opened to see the reality of their Master, Jesus Christ. The glory of Jesus was with them all the time, but they could not see his glory until God opened their eyes, their hearts, and their minds here on Mount Tabor.

"We also need to have God transfigure not only our eyes, but also our tongues and our hands so that we use them to bless rather than to curse people."

We were quiet together for a while, contemplating the beauty of Christ and how God gives us the gift of transfiguration in our daily lives.

"You all know about the kind of icon that is painted on wood," I said, "but I wonder if you know about the other kind of icon." Byzantine Christians use icons as an avenue of prayer to God. Icons are pictures of Jesus, Mary, and the saints beautifully painted on wood, sometimes with precious metals carved to be halos around the heads or to be the clothing. Every Byzantine home has at least one icon, usually of the Virgin Mary, and it is given a place of honor in the house.

The very first icon any iconographer paints is the Icon of the Transfiguration of Christ. Before beginning this or any other icon, the artist meditates, praying that God will transfigure the paints, brushes, and person of the artist. The prayer asks that humans who gaze at the icon will be transfigured by the power of the Holy Spirit through this particular visualization of God's love.

"The true icon is your neighbor," I explained to my companions on Mount Tabor, "the human being who has been created in the image and with the likeness of God. How beautiful it is when our eyes are transfigured and we see that our neighbor is the icon of God, and that you, and you, and I—we are all the icons of God. How serious it is when we hate the image of God, whoever that may be, whether a Jew or a Palestinian. How serious it is when we cannot go and say, 'I am sorry about the icon of God who was hurt by my behavior.' We

46

all need to be transfigured so we can recognize the glory of God in one another."

We remained on Mount Tabor until late in the afternoon, praying, singing, and meditating. In a beautiful calmness, we drove back down the winding road to the plain and then up the smaller hill on which Nazareth is built.

I pointed out the small Orthodox church that covers an ancient well from the time of Jesus, a well Mary must have used. I showed my companions the Melkite Catholic seminary on the hill, where I had attended secondary school, and the chapel where I had been ordained. As we approached the convent of the Sisters of St. Joseph, I stopped to show the young women where nuns of this order are trained and where they live.

"You know about Sister Miriam from Ibillin, don't you?" I asked. They all nodded. Her picture was everywhere in the village. Miriam Bawardy had lived in Ibillin as a child about seventy-five years earlier. Eventually she became a Carmelite nun and took the name of Miriam (Mary), the Sister of Jesus Crucified. People also called her "the little Arab." Sister Miriam established Carmelite orders and built convents in Palestine and India. While carrying buckets of water to the workers building a convent in Bethlehem, she fell and broke both legs. Gangrene set in, and she died at the age of thirty-three. It is said that when she died, the bells rang in Bethlehem, Ibillin, and many other places.

After her death Sister Miriam was simply called "the saint" in Ibillin. Whenever the people thought of her, they thought of God. The villagers began to light candles and pray at the ruins of her parents' house in Ibillin. Hundreds of candles and piles of frankincense are found in that place every evening, the remnants of daily prayers offered to God.

Looking at the convent's huge stone walls, I felt the familiar disgust I had experienced as a schoolboy there in Nazareth. Goodness, I used to say, with these outside walls I could build a whole village for the people of Biram. Why is the church identifying with wealth, power, and prestige? Does that reflect

Jesus Christ, the Man from Galilee? I know that the people who live behind these walls pray, study, and worship, but they are not helping poor people in their daily lives. It was truly a scandal to me.

I started the engine of my car, wanting to leave this place, when an idea occurred to me. Many nuns were just sitting inside those walls. What if I invited two of them to come to Ibillin and help me minister to the people there? Would any of them agree to do that? *Well,* I thought as I drove toward Ibillin, *I must talk to Mother Josephat soon.*

Chapter 7

Go Visit Every Home!

"So what happened? What did the bishop say?" I was standing in front of the provincial mother's desk in St. Joseph's Convent in Nazareth.

Mother Josephat sniffed and pursed her lips. "Well, I have sad news. I tried to convince the bishop to send two nuns to Ibillin, as you suggested, but when he heard there were no Roman Catholics in the village nor any hope the nuns would create any, he denied the request."

I shook my head, feeling my hopefulness drain away. "This man has no vision, and what is worse, he does not put the needs of the people first."

Three days after I stared at the thick, outside walls of the convent, I had spoken with Mother Josephat about my great love and concern for the people in the villages of Galilee, pointing out that they had been abandoned by almost everybody, including the Church. "Wouldn't it be wonderful if two nuns from this convent could help me teach the children Bible stories and how to sing the liturgy? And they could make home visits and help the women and girls learn to sew."

Mother Josephat had been sympathetic and saw a good opportunity for the nuns. "However, Abuna," she had said, "I must ask our bishop for permission."

My heart sank, but Mother Josephat had been encouraging, saying it was just a matter of protocol. We had set a date for the next week when the bishop would be in Nazareth and the subject could be discussed. Now, however, I saw all the wonderful possibilities evaporating.

"Well, Mother Josephat, what will you do?"

The provincial mother stood up behind her desk. "Abuna Elias, the bishop was very clear in his refusal to allow two nuns to come to Ibillin. I cannot disobey him in that." I nodded, understanding her situation. "So, Abuna, I will send you *three* nuns!"

My mouth dropped open. "What? *What?* You will?"

Mother Josephat laughed at my reaction. "Yes, I will send three nuns to Ibillin. I know the need is very great. Besides, I think some of these women are getting too stuffy in their thinking and need to be spiritually renewed by a pastoral life. We have much to learn from the Christian villages. Jesus was also a simple villager. I hope the nuns will be able to meet Jesus in the village."

Very early the next Sunday I arrived at the convent to take the nuns to Ibillin. Mother Josephat brought me to a sitting room and introduced me to the three women dressed in identical gray habits. "Abuna, I want you to meet Mère Macaire, Sister Gislaine, and Sister Nazarena. Sisters, this is Abuna Elias Chacour, with whom you will work in the village of Ibillin."

I shook hands with each of the nuns.

Mère Macaire was stately in her bearing with a certain remoteness in her expression, the result of once having been mother superior of a convent, I learned later. She was considerably older than the other nuns.

Sister Gislaine was short, rather rotund, and wore a big smile. She seemed very intelligent. I would soon discover her unlimited generosity and unshakable faith.

Sister Nazarena was of medium height and very thin. Her smile was delightful and she had a great love for children. Later I learned her health was poor, and she sometimes was hospitalized for stomach disorders.

"Welcome!" I said. "We are looking forward to your visit to Ibillin."

Mère Macaire spoke immediately. "Is it agreed that after the liturgy you will bring us back to the convent right away?"

I was shocked. I had expected the nuns to spend the whole day in Ibillin and even, perhaps, to spend the night so they could go visiting homes on Monday. I looked at Mother Josephat in some bewilderment.

The provincial mother just smiled reassuringly at me and nodded her head as if to say, "Go ahead, do it."

"That's fine," I said to the three nuns, who looked much happier once their return was settled. "Come, I will take you to Ibillin to pray."

Sure enough, immediately after the liturgy the nuns got in my car to be driven back to Nazareth, waiting impatiently while I greeted everyone. I was extremely irritated, because I did not have time to be a driver to transport nuns all the way from Nazareth just to pray and then to return home. But I remembered Mother Josephat's smile and nod, and decided to hold my tongue. I also prayed that the Holy Spirit would act—and fast!

The following Sundays the nuns behaved the same way. Then, on the sixth Sunday, Mère Macaire announced, "Well, Abuna, perhaps we can afford to stay after the liturgy to get acquainted. The people look kind enough."

"Fine, Mère Macaire," I said, trying to keep from smiling too broadly.

After the liturgy the nuns sat with me in my room, and soon the village people came to visit, bearing gifts. "Abuna, we know that the nuns are staying with you, so we are bringing our food to share with you," one woman said.

The nuns were absolutely delighted at the outpouring of love and affection. When I finally took them back to the convent in the evening, they were already telling me they would stay again the next Sunday. I suggested they visit the homes of the people, assuring them they need only go to the homes of "good Christian families." They were hesitant but willing to consider the radical new step.

It was Sister Gislaine who received a baptism by fire in village visitation a few weeks later. I told her on Palm Sunday that I would visit all the Melkite families on Easter and invited her to join me.

"Come, Sister Gislaine," I said after the big celebration of the Divine Liturgy on Easter Sunday. "We have many homes to visit today."

"I am ready, Abuna," she said, smiling. Her gray habit and veil were crisp and without a wrinkle. "Let's go."

And so began the round of Easter visits that took us to more than sixty homes in Ibillin in one day. Up rocky hills, down pebbly, dusty roads, across fields, under olive trees, through herds of sheep and goats we went, finding our Melkite families and saying, "Christ is risen!" They would answer, "He is truly risen!" Then they would give us a cookie or two. We would say, "We'll see you next Sunday in church," and off we'd go to another home, bringing our greetings and invitation.

By seven o'clock in the evening we had come away from the last home and were walking slowly back to the parish house.

"Well, what do you think, Sister Gislaine?" I asked. "Was it a good day visiting the families?" She did not answer. "Did you have a good time?"

When she still did not answer, I stopped and looked around. Sister Gislaine had lagged behind me, walking very slowly, puffing. Her face was flushed and her lovely gray habit was rumpled and disarrayed. Her shoes were covered with dust and her veil was askew on her head. I walked back down the hill to take her arm.

"Are you all right, Sister Gislaine? You look exhausted."

"I *am* exhausted, Abuna," she said, gasping. "Yes, it was a good day, but I can barely go another step." Arm in arm, we trudged up the hill to the parish house. After resting awhile and quenching her thirst with lots of water, Sister Gislaine climbed into my car with the other two nuns. She promptly fell asleep on the short ride to Nazareth.

But I was jubilant. We had visited every Melkite family in Ibillin on Easter Sunday 1967! The people knew that Christ had risen from the dead, and now they also knew that Abuna Elias and Sister Gislaine loved them so much they had come to their houses to greet them on this Resurrection Day.

One Sunday about three months later, when I came to transport the nuns to Ibillin they were carrying their suitcases. They had decided to live in the village. Mother Josephat waved goodbye, beaming her approval. It seemed there was life beyond the convent walls after all.

"You can sleep here," I told the nuns as we stood in my room.

"But, Abuna," Sister Nazarena said, looking around, "where will *you* sleep?"

"Don't worry at all. I have a place to sleep. This room and the kitchen are all for you. Welcome!"

That night I was once again in the backseat of my Volkswagen, trying to get reasonably comfortable. But I didn't mind. The nuns were staying in the village, and now much work could be done in this community. After I had slept in the car or on church benches for several months, the community helped me build an extra room on the parish house.

"Who wants to come with me for wake-up calls?" I asked the nuns early one Sunday morning. Sisters Gislaine and Nazarena decided to accompany me.

"*Salaam alekhum,*" I called, knocking loudly on Abu Nimer's door. "Wake up, it is eight o'clock. In one hour I will celebrate the liturgy, and I want you and your family to join me."

Abu Nimer stuck his sleepy head out the window and waved his hand as the nuns and I continued down the street.

"Hello, Abu Mouheeb," I said to a man standing in his doorway as we passed. "Soon I'll be ringing the bell for the liturgy. The nuns and I will be waiting to see you and your family at prayer."

"Wake up, wake up!" the nuns called at the next house. "We are all waiting for you to pray. You are all invited to sip coffee with us afterward."

Every Sunday after the liturgy people visited us, often bringing cookies and candies to share with one another while they enjoyed the coffee and friendly atmosphere the nuns provided. The Spirit was at work, and the family was gathering.

The nuns quickly learned that I regarded visitation as a holy task. "We are going to create a new reality in Ibillin," I told them shortly after they arrived. "We will systematically visit every family in our Melkite community. Our message is that we need each other, we belong together, and we love each other."

During the nuns' first year in Ibillin we visited each Melkite family four times and established a workable schedule. The nuns were comfortable with this arrangement. Too comfortable, I thought.

"Today we will visit Um Mousa and Um Khalid," I announced.

"But, Abuna, they are not Melkites," Mère Macaire protested. "We visit only Melkite families."

"You have visited only Melkite families until now, Sister, but today you will begin visiting the Orthodox families, too. Abuna Ibrahim is happy to have you do that. I already told him you would."

"But . . . but they are *Orthodox!*" Sister Nazarena's eyes were very wide. "What will we say to them?"

"They are Christians just like you, Sister. And they are waiting for you to come." I stood up and walked toward the door. "I will return in ten minutes, and we can begin our visits."

"Well!" I heard Mère Macaire snort as soon as I was outside. "Next thing you know he will ask us to visit *Muslim* families!"

I poked my head back through the doorway and grinned at the startled nuns. "Next week, Sisters! Next week!"

One day in late fall 1967 the rain fell steadily, sending streams of water down the Ibillin hill. During the night the storm worsened. I was awakened by fierce lightning cracks and nearly simultaneous roars of thunder. I lay on my mat, grateful to be back in the parish house, listening to the storm pound the village.

Suddenly there was an enormous crash, and the room was lighted as if it were noontime. I jumped to my feet and pulled on my clothes. Something nearby had been hit by lightning. *O God, was it the church?*

I ran out into the storm, fearing I would see a pile of stones where the church had stood, but the building was untouched. Hearing cries of alarm on the other side of the hill, I slipped and slid through the mud that had been a street the day before.

"What is it?" I shouted when I found Habib and several other men. "What was hit?" They pointed toward the mosque, and we stood together staring at the gaping split in the domed roof.

Many other men were gathering now, including Ibillin's Muslim clergyman, Sheikh Ahmad, or Abu Muhammad. He pounded his chest in grief, as did the other Muslim men. The Christians tried to comfort them, feeling shock and grief themselves. After a while we dispersed, promising to come back in the daylight to assess the damage.

The children made mud fortresses and castles the next day, as the adults slowly walked around the mosque, shaking their heads. In the sunlight it was apparent that the damage was extensive.

"Abu Muhammad, I am so sorry about the mosque," I told the sheikh when I found him moving some of the rubble aside. I helped him push a big block of stone out of the way.

"Thank you, Abuna Elias," the sheikh said, pausing to wipe perspiration from his worried face with his handkerchief. "This is such a shock. Yesterday we were praying here, and today the mosque is nearly destroyed."

"Well, why don't you come and pray in the Melkite church?"

The sheikh looked unbelievingly at me. "What? You invite us to pray in your church?"

"Yes, why not?"

"But we are Muslims, not Christians."

"So what? You praise God during your prayers, don't you?"

"Yes, of course."

"I do not pray better than you do, Abu Muhammad. You are welcome to use our church for your prayers until the mosque can be repaired."

From that moment the relations between Christians and Muslims in Ibillin were vastly improved.

Earlier in 1967 several of us from the Melkite and Orthodox communities had collected funds to enlarge and repair the deteriorating Orthodox church. The wall around the Christian cemetery was also repaired so the animals could not wander in. The remaining funds were left with me.

The lightning strike occasioned the writing of my first circular letter to the villagers.

Thank you for your contributions to repair the Orthodox church and to build a wall around the cemetery. I still have some money left, and since I know how tolerant you are, my Christian friends, and how loving you are for your Muslim brothers and sisters, I have used it to order building materials to reconstruct the mosque.

"The Christian priest is giving us some money to reconstruct our mosque," the Muslim people said. "It is a shame if we do not help him to enlarge and repair the mosque." Together the Christians and Muslims reconstructed the mosque, built a huge wall around it, and hung the main, steel gate on which is written in Arabic *Allahu akbar*, God is great.

"We have been in almost all the homes in the village now," Sister Nazarena said one noon after dinner, "and we have noticed a great need."

"A very great need," Sister Gislaine emphasized.

Mère Macaire nodded.

"Abuna, we would like to start a kindergarten for the small children of the village," Sister Nazarena said, her words tumbling out. "There are so many of them, and they just play in the streets and the fields until they go to the first level of school."

"Abuna, it would be so beneficial for them if they could attend a kindergarten daily. They could learn singing, drawing, games, Bible stories, numbers, letters." Sister Gislaine was counting the things on her fingers. "The children are so bright and alert, but their mothers are busy and don't have time to teach them all these things."

"That's why *we* would like to teach them, Abuna. May we start a kindergarten here in the parish house?" Sister Nazarena ran out of breath.

Mother Josephat, I wish you could be here, I exulted. *This is what I have been praying for, hoping for, all these months!* The nuns had become increasingly innovative and daring, but this! This idea for a kindergarten took desire, commitment, and courage!

I could no longer conceal the huge smile that insisted on covering my face.

The nuns jumped up, squealing like schoolgirls. "It's all right? We can do it?" They rushed toward me.

"Absolutely! It's a wonderful idea! When can you start?"

Any answers were drowned out in the noisy joy surrounding me.

Chapter 8

We Young Priests

In 1967 I began attending Hebrew University in Jerusalem. Bishop Hakim asked me to do so, saying he wanted me to learn more about the Jewish Bible and theology. To cover the tuition I gave private lessons and public lectures on Christian theology at the university and also received a scholarship. Now, late in 1969, I was nearing graduation with a master's degree, the first Palestinian and the first Christian priest to earn a degree at Hebrew University in Bible and in Talmud.

The two years at the university had been exciting for me but also very tiring. I would spend a few days in school in Jerusalem and then return to Ibillin to work with the people on our many projects.

One morning Abu Yacub, a member of our church, came to visit me as I was preparing a lecture. He seated himself comfortably beside my desk and loosened his *keffiyeh*.

"Abuna, last Sunday in church you said that whenever we pass by your door and find it open, we are welcome to come in and visit. So here I am."

"This is good," I replied, glancing sidelong at my unfinished lecture.

Abu Yacub told me news about his health, his land, and his donkey. Soon he began repeating some of the stories. Then he fell silent. It was ten-thirty, then eleven o'clock. He had nothing more to say yet he continued to sit by my desk. The unwritten rules of Palestinian hospitality required me to be a good host for as long as my guest wished to stay. Eleven-thirty, twelve o'clock noon.

Finally he spoke again. "Abuna, I know you are bored with me."

"No, no, Abu Yacub. I am not bored with you, but today I must prepare a lecture to give to university professors, and it is very difficult."

"I know that, too, Abuna," the old man said, leaning his elbow on my desk. "That is why I am here. We do not want you to work anymore. What you know is enough for us. We do not want you to spoil your eyes."

I could not help but laugh. What a crazy man! What a loving man! He was trying to help me by stopping what I wanted to do for these people. What an idiot man! What a good man!

"Yes, Abu Yacub. I appreciate that so much."

The telephone call had come at nine-thirty as I was preparing to leave for my morning classes at the university in my final semester.

"Abuna Elias? This is the son of Abuna Ibrahim. I am sorry to bother you there in Jerusalem, but my family and I want you to know that Father died this morning."

Palestinian funerals and burials are always held within a few hours of death. The body is washed and prepared for burial. Family and friends quickly gather to comfort the mourners and to walk in a procession with the body, which is wrapped in a shroud and carried in a wooden box on the shoulders of several men. First the people take the body to the church for the funeral, then to the cemetery for burial.

Abuna Ibrahim's funeral would be in the afternoon of this late fall day in 1969. I wanted very much to say goodbye to my dear old friend and be part of the community farewell.

Just a year and a half earlier on Good Friday 1968 I had invited Abuna Ibrahim and the Greek Orthodox community to worship with the Melkites in our church. This was a radical step because of the past enmity in Ibillin and also because of the larger history of the Greek Orthodox and the Greek Catholic churches. The "royalists," or Melkites, were followers of the king in Constantinople who allied with the pope in Rome in the eleventh century. The Christians who remained loyal to the patriarch of Constantinople were the Orthodox. To this day the Orthodox regard the Melkites as traitors, while the Melkites regard the much larger Orthodox church with suspicion and fear. Only as Abuna Ibrahim and I gradually came to be friends and partner priests in Ibillin had the old walls of bitterness, hatred, and fear come down. By Good Friday 1968 it was possible to worship together.

Orthodox and Melkite people jammed into our small church. Abuna Ibrahim sat in the front row beaming at me as I led the prayers. When the liturgy was finished, I helped him step up into the central archway, facing the people. Abuna Ibrahim was trembling with excitement, his eyes bright.

"Praise to God, my brothers and sisters! We are experiencing a miracle! I have not dared put my foot on this church property or in this church building for nearly twenty years. And today I am invited to preach to you all, Orthodox and Melkite alike." Many of the people were weeping.

"Abuna Elias," the old priest said, turning to me, "I love you. I wish I had twenty years to work with you here in the village. I want you to know that we young priests are not like those old-fashioned, closed-minded priests. We young priests, we love the Church. We want it to be united. That's why I consider your church to be my church. And I want you to think of my church as your church." The people applauded their approval as I stepped up into the archway to embrace my old colleague and friend.

Quickly I drove out of Jerusalem and began the three-hour journey to Ibillin. Driving past the Latrun monastery, I remembered the nearby village of Imwas (Emmaus), destroyed in 1967. Since 1948, 385 Palestinian villages had been destroyed inside Israel, reinforcing the myth of "an empty land." The remaining Palestinian villages, less than one hundred of them, were primarily in Galilee.[1]

The Palestinians who did not leave Israel in 1948 were restricted to their remaining villages, denied communication with other villages, and deprived of much of their leadership. They were trying to accommodate Palestinian refugees from destroyed villages, all the while seeing much of their farming land confiscated and worrying about the future of their own villages. In the late sixties the government eased the restrictions on Arab Israeli travel inside the country, but the confiscation of village land by the Israeli government continued, and the Palestinian villages in Galilee received little or no government assistance, help readily available to neighboring Jewish towns and *kibbutzim*.

Although the Palestinians inside Israel were Israeli citizens, it was second- and third-class citizenship. Many rights and privileges belonging to Jewish Israelis were usually denied to Arab Israelis, including the right to equal education, housing, jobs, and social and recreational facilities. The goal seemed to be the isolation and dependence of the Arabs inside Israel.[2]

I had undertaken a study of the Palestinian villages in Galilee in 1968 and discovered that 75 percent of the people were below twenty-eight years of age. Fifty percent were below fourteen years. I quickly saw that nothing at all was being done for this young generation. The children and teenagers of the villages, some of whom were in school and others of whom did not continue after the eighth grade because of the absence of school facilities, idled away many empty hours every day, usually playing in the dusty streets. Their human rights, dignity, and future were being suppressed and even eliminated. I found confusion, despair, bitterness, and much fear among the Palestinian young people, including those from Ibillin.

I became determined to change the current situation and the future for the Palestinian young people in Galilee. Undoubtedly I was reliving my own childhood when I was a refugee from Biram at the age of eight, when I lived in one room in Jish with eleven members of my family, when I played in the dusty streets of Jish and tried to learn in the woefully inadequate school. By the determination of my father and the grace of God, I had been able to leave Jish at the age of twelve and begin my education, which led to Paris and the priesthood. But I was a rarity. Nearly every other young adult my age was trapped in the villages with little education and poor prospects for the future. I spent much time in prayer asking God to give me the wisdom, opportunities, and resources to create a new reality for the children, for my people.

Instinctively I had known that home visitation, education, love, and reconciliation were essential for the people's dignity and sense of community, and therefore as a priest I had practiced these things and asked the nuns to do so, too. But now . . . now I could see what my priesthood was all about. I was to provide the Palestinian young people in Galilee with opportunities for today as well as possibilities and goals for tomorrow, for the future. My mind was overflowing with ideas.

One Sunday I made a special announcement at the close of the liturgy. "My friends, I am happy to tell you that a small library has now been established here in Ibillin. A few hundred books are in my room at the parish house, and you are all welcome to come and check out books, particularly the young people. Also, we need book donations so if any of you have books at home that you would like to contribute, please bring them to me."

The "Ibillin Public Library" was stocked with my own books collected during my school years. As a child I never had a book. My father told me to pick up anything in the streets with printing on it, and I collected scraps of paper I found, reading the words over and over. In the Bishop's School in Haifa I devoured the books in the small library, pleading for more time in the evening to read. My personal library was my treasure, but now I wanted to give it away to the young people of Ibillin.

Soon books and money were donated to the library. The children checked out books every day, proudly carrying them in the streets. I had discovered a tremendous thirst and hunger to read, to learn, to know, and to be educated, not only among the children but among the adults as well.

The nuns' kindergarten was proving to be a big success, beginning with twenty children and soon expanding to fifty. Two more rooms had recently been added to the parish house to give the nuns private quarters, but I was again sleeping in my car. My room was the kindergarten room during the day, the library in the afternoon and evening, and a storage room at night. The situation was impossible.

A simple, two-room kindergarten building was soon constructed near the church, enabling us to handle seventy children, but still we were crowded. The blessing for me was that I could once again use the Ibillin Public Library as my office and bedroom.

News of the library, kindergarten, story hours, Bible classes, and field trips soon filtered into the other Palestinian villages in Galilee. Requests began arriving for assistance to start similar programs in those places, but I had no extra resources. Perhaps someday there would be a miracle so I could help all the villages, but that time had not yet come.

The crowd outside Abuna Ibrahim's house was enormous. Orthodox and Melkite Christians as well as many Muslims from all over Galilee had gathered in the yard and the street to pay their respects and homage to the beloved priest. The Orthodox bishop with about twenty-five Orthodox priests, all dressed in black cassocks and wearing their flat-topped hats, were seated in an elevated place of honor.

I greeted Abuna Ibrahim's sons, and we embraced and wept together. After hugging the grandchildren, I turned to the bishop and the retinue of priests. "Peace be with you, your excellency," I said to the bishop, who motioned me to sit beside him.

The bishop leaned close to me to speak with more privacy. "Abuna Elias, it is good to see you. But we have a problem, I'm afraid. I have a letter here from the patriarch." The bishop pulled a paper from inside his robe and then hesitated, frowning in his beard. "It is a rather difficult time . . . yet it is also an ideal time to distribute the orders of the patriarch because there are Orthodox people here from all over Galilee." He glanced at the crowd, which, from this elevated vantage point, could be easily numbered at more than two thousand people.

"What are the patriarch's orders?"

"His orders are that Orthodox Christians must not pray with any other Christians, whether in their own or in other churches. Here, read it for yourself."

I took the letter and quickly scanned it. The orders were dreadful, almost unbelievable. The Greek Orthodox patriarch was actually forbidding his people to worship with any non-Orthodox Christians.

"This is terrible, terrible!" I cried. "Surely you will not obey this order?"

"It is the will of the patriarch. There is no choice, Abuna."

"But this will destroy the funeral, the burial, and even the legacy of this good, holy priest who worked so hard in Ibillin to bring people together! Don't you understand? The Orthodox and Melkite Christians in this village *love* each other and they work together, just as Abuna Ibrahim and I worked together. Such an order is horrible anywhere and it is absolutely unthinkable in Ibillin, especially on this day." My whole body was quivering and my voice was rising in volume and intensity.

The Orthodox bishop took my arm, speaking in low, confidential tones. "Look, Abuna Elias, I do not want to have any trouble here, but I must distribute the patriarch's letter."

I took a deep breath, trying to quiet my turbulent thoughts. "Bishop, may I say one more thing before you distribute this letter?"

"Fine, say what you want," he said, looking relieved.

I walked out to the edge of the elevated area and shouted to the thousands of people, who quieted immediately. "We have gathered to pay our respects to Abuna Ibrahim and to console his family in the time of their sorrow. This priest who is now dead, this precious Abuna Ibrahim who was beloved by us all—he was not only the Orthodox priest, my friends. He was the priest of Ibillin, venerated by Muslims, Melkites, and Orthodox alike."

A murmur of agreement rippled through the crowd. Several priests began whispering to the bishop.

"That is why, to give Abuna Ibrahim due honors and to respect him as he deserves, I propose that we process with his body first to the Melkite church and celebrate his funeral there, and then take his body to the Orthodox church and celebrate again before he is buried."

The people began to applaud and shout their approval. "That is what Abuna Ibrahim would have wanted! We are one church in Ibillin!"

When I returned to my seat by the bishop, he was glowering at me. "You are very good at making proposals, Abuna Elias. Now what do you propose I do with the letter of the patriarch?"

64

"Leave it until after the funeral, bishop. Wait until the body is in the ground. Then do whatever you want with that damnable letter."

After the two funeral liturgies had been sung, Abuna Ibrahim was buried in the Orthodox churchyard, right beside the entrance, a place of great honor and respect. There everyone would remember the beloved priest, praising and thanking the Lord for Abuna Ibrahim's life and memory.

Tonight I am the only Christian priest in Ibillin, I thought, stretching out on my bed well after midnight. *My friend is gone.* Hot tears of sorrow, anger, and pain spilled over and I sobbed into my pillow. I had been strong for everybody else all day. I wept for a long time.

Finally I sat on the edge of the bed and blew my nose. My sinuses were clogged, and I sounded like a bellowing cow. Suddenly a wave of dizziness, nausea, and disorientation swept over me. I grabbed the side of the bed for support. *O God, it's happening again. What is wrong with me?*

Gradually the symptoms subsided, and I carefully lay down. These spells were occurring more and more often. *They must be due to the huge work load I am carrying in Ibillin and Jerusalem,* I thought, *and the long, tense drive back to the village today would have made anyone dizzy.*

I slept, only to dream. I was leading the Divine Liturgy, and the Melkite children were heartily singing the responses, just as Sister Nazarena had taught them. The adults were starting to sing, too. It was beautiful, and I felt happy. When it was time for the Eucharist, everyone came to receive Holy Communion, led by the children. My poor Responsible was watching from the back of the church. As in real life, he had lost his power over the people and seemed lonesome. I kept beckoning him to join us, but he ignored me. Then I saw Faraj come into the church. He looked dreadfully ill, and I suddenly remembered how worried I had been about him at the last priests' retreat in Nazareth. What was the matter with my dear friend? I struggled to reach Faraj but couldn't seem to move through the huge group of communing people. I must go to him, I must . . .

65

I awoke with a start, drenched with perspiration, tingling all over. *O God, I am exhausted. I am sick. Have you brought me this far to abandon me? Is it time for me to leave Ibillin? If so, where should I go? What do you want me to do?*

No answers came. God, as usual, was silent. After a long while I slept once again.

Chapter 9

Escape

The letter had been read so often it looked and felt like a soft piece of cloth. The Institute of Bossey in Geneva, Switzerland, was inviting me to be a guest professor in Christian theology and comparative religions for one year. I savored the invitation for many days in the spring of 1970.

But how could I leave Ibillin? After years of struggle I was now fully accepted as priest and friend. The library, the kindergarten, and various youth activities were in full swing, and we hoped to build a community center. Things were going very well.

I myself, however, was not at all well. The dizziness was occurring frequently, but I had no money to go to a doctor. Emotionally I felt I could no longer bear the pain and pressure of being a Palestinian living in Israel, suffering under a political system that didn't want me there.

I knew of the suffering the Jewish people had experienced in Europe during the Second World War, how they had been without a homeland for nearly nineteen hundred years, and that our land of Palestine had been home to them before the Romans drove them out, but I also knew other things:

- that my Palestinian ancestors had been in this land before the Iraqi Gentile Abraham arrived twenty centuries before Christ;
- that Jews and Gentiles alike had been in this land when Jesus of Nazareth lived here, easily noted in all the gospel accounts;
- that my ancestors, like the Jews, had loved and cherished this land, planting their olive and fig trees that still

nourished us twenty centuries after Jesus Christ had
walked in these paths and fields;
and that we as Palestinians had not been responsible for
the suffering of the Jews in Europe, yet we were the ones
who were chased out of our land and made to suffer so
the world could soothe its conscience and pretend to
repair the evil done against the Jews.

I did not begrudge a home to the Jews. As my father and
our friends and relatives in Biram had often said, *"Ahlan
wassahlan,* welcome to our home, our Jewish friends. We love to
have you here as our neighbors and compatriots. We sorrow
with you in your pain and rejoice in your freedom, but that
welcome does not entitle you to take our lands and villages away
from us, to threaten us and even kill our people, to become lord
and master over us, consigning us to slavery, dispossession, and
nonexistence. Come, let us be brothers and sisters together in
this beautiful land in which all of us have history and roots.
There is room enough for all of us. Aren't we the co-persecuted
brothers and sisters?"

Israel was established on the principles of modern Zionism,
which wanted a state in which Jewish people could be protected
and in charge of their own destiny. By its nature, however,
Zionism calls for fundamentalism, radicalism. It is built on a
racial theory, and anything based on race or on blood, like
nationhood, peoplehood, or homeland, always risks becoming
racist. Racist thinking separates one group of people from
others, favors that group over and against people who are
different, and, when a real or imagined threat to the favored
people is perceived, can justify any activity to assure their safety
and security.

Today, with the state of Israel a reality, individual Jews,
Jewish groups, and the Israeli government must practice self-
criticism so that Zionism does not become racist, a new expression of the "race of lords," regarding one group of people as
superior to all others. The world witnessed that among the
Greeks and the Romans. Palestinians were slaves under the
Ottoman Turks, who saw themselves as lords. Hitler brought
this theory to a peak of horror when he placed the Aryan race
above all others. There are only a few small steps between

protecting and championing an oppressed group of people and proclaiming the rights of that group as more important than the rights of others. What appears to be a just necessity at one point can become blind arrogance later if not continually subjected to balanced, realistic scrutiny and judgment.

Human worth, human qualities, are much more important than Jewish, Palestinian, or American nationalism, peoplehood, or land. Sometimes it seems to me that Zionism pushes the Jews to *Zionize* themselves rather than *humanize* themselves. When a particular group is blinded with its own identity, its thinking and perceptions can become distorted through an intellectual game of progression: "We are different. It is normal that other people persecute us and hate us because we are different from them. We are better than they are; they are lower than we are. We are of more value, they are of less value." This thinking is extremely dangerous.

It has always been my prayer that the Jews would never fall into this dangerous trap, because people commit suicide when they believe in their pure blood. They kill others with themselves, pushing the concept of their rightness and value above every other consideration. No, I did not begrudge a home to the Jews, but I wanted my own home, too, and in 1970 I had become weary of trying to justify my existence.

Bishop Hakim had become the Melkite patriarch in Beirut, and we in Galilee now had a new bishop, Joseph Raya, a man whom I respected. Nevertheless, the pastoral carelessness within my own Melkite church was becoming unbearable. I fought against the emphasis on personal and political status, on money and prestige, but it felt like a losing battle.

Geneva, Switzerland, was looking better to me all the time.

After the fortieth-day remembrance of Abuna Ibrahim's death, I met with the Orthodox Christian elders at their church.

"I am sorry, but I am the only priest in the village now," I said. "I know your patriarch has told you not to pray with us, but I feel responsible to care for your souls."

"We are not going to pay any attention to that order, Abuna Elias," Abu Kamil said. "We are one Christian family here in

Ibillin, and we know you will be priest to us as well as to the Melkites."

"Yes, I am ready to serve you as long as I live, my friends, but as willing as I am to help you, this arrangement cannot work always. With over 3,000 members in your community you need a priest of your own to celebrate Sunday mass and all the weddings, funerals, and baptisms."

"You are right, Abuna Elias, but the bishop has no priest available, and we know of no new candidate. What can we do except depend on you?"

"Well, there may be another way." I then told them I had spoken with Awad Awad, a devoted, pious Orthodox man in Ibillin who was willing to be a priest candidate. The elders were happy with the choice and decided to circulate the petition I had written. More than 350 people signed it, and the Orthodox patriarch agreed to ordain the young Ibillin farmer, married with eight children, not knowing I was the troublesome boy who had arranged the matter.

Awad Awad was ordained in Jerusalem, and within two weeks was back in Ibillin as Abuna Awad with a new beard and a new cassock. He could sing the liturgy, but had had no other preparation.

One day Abuna Awad sat by my desk, smiling. "Abuna Elias, will you teach me everything you know about theology and philosophy?. You're the reason I am a priest so I think you must teach me."

I thought there was a better way to help this new priest. "Abuna Awad, have you ever read the entire New Testament, page to page?"

"No, but I have heard many passages read in church."

"This is excellent," I said, smiling at my new colleague. "If you like, I know a way to teach you theology and philosophy."

"Wonderful! How is that?"

"I will come to your home every day, and we will read the New Testament from beginning to end, discussing it as we go."

In late 1969 and early 1970 Abuna Awad and I studied together. It was a time of grace for me, a heavenly gift, reading together the good news about our Champion and Compatriot, Jesus Christ. Many evenings the priest and his wife prepared my dinner, trying to repay me for the lessons, but, in fact, I received much more from this humble, serene, and transparent man than I ever gave him.

Every Saturday now, Abuna Awad's wife bakes the communion bread for the Orthodox church. As a continuing gift of gratitude she also bakes the bread for the Melkites' celebration of the Holy Eucharist. Each Sunday in our liturgy I pray for that priest, his wife, and their children.

Abuna Awad and I often celebrate weddings and funerals together, and in June when Abuna Awad goes to tend his cucumber fields, the Orthodox people come to pray with the Melkites. When I need to be out of town, the Melkites go to pray at the Orthodox church. I believe that Ibillin is the only place in the world where Orthodox and Melkite Christians are in fellowship.

During my two years of study and teaching at Hebrew University people wanted to know me, to have me in their meetings and on their panels. One of the tremendous gifts I received was the friendship of certain Jewish students and professors. One family in particular welcomed me into their home, and our relationship was always that of human beings who enjoyed and treasured each other. I enjoyed playing with the children in that Jewish family, watching them grow into strong, sensitive young people.

When I finally graduated at the end of 1969, the university honored me and then issued an international press release describing my life and this first-time event of a Palestinian Christian priest earning a master's degree in Bible and Talmudic studies. The resultant publicity connected me with heretofore unknown family in other parts of the world and also brought invitations to speak at various conferences, the beginning of my international relations. Now in the spring of 1970, I was struggling to decide whether to accept or reject the invitation to teach in Geneva.

One morning the issue was decided for me when my health broke. I could not get out of bed because I could not completely wake up. Only when Sister Gislaine knocked at my door did I rally enough to tell her I was all right. But I was not all right, and

I actually wondered if I was sick unto death. Money or no money, I knew I must go to the doctor in Nazareth.

"How did you get to the hospital, Abuna?" the doctor asked as he examined me.

"I drove myself in my car."

"My God, you must be insane! If you don't care for your own life, you should at least care for the lives of others. You are not far from collapsing and dying, Abuna. If your blood pressure were just a few degrees lower, you *would* be dead. You must stay here in the hospital so we can raise your pressure and find out why it has dropped like this."

I was so sick and weak that I did everything they told me to do. After three days I felt better and began worrying about the expense of the hospital room, sixty pounds per day (about thirty dollars U.S.). I had to go home. The doctor had ordered more tests and said I should be hospitalized for a week, but it was impossible. I had no money to pay what I already owed. Besides, the doctor said I was debilitated because I was not eating often enough nor eating the right kinds of food. I also needed to sleep more, he said. Goodness, those things I could do in Ibillin.

"Well, the doctor has liberated me," I said to the receptionist in the hospital lobby, dressed in my cassock and smiling my healthiest smile. She hurriedly checked some lists and looked confused, but I kept moving toward the door. "I'll be sending the money for the bill very soon." I waved at her and went outside. Aha! I had escaped.

But I was celebrating too soon. Just as I drove my car out of the parking lot, Sister Gislaine arrived and saw me. "Abuna! Where are you going? I am coming to visit you!"

"I am healed now, all recovered," I called to her, stepping on the accelerator and making my getaway.

The day after Pentecost in June 1970 I left Ibillin to teach for one year in Geneva. A procession of thirty-five cars filled with people from the village accompanied me to Ben Gurion Airport. Before my plane left, we prayed and wept together, and I felt like the Apostle Paul saying goodbye to the elders at Ephesus. I wanted to teach in Geneva, leaving the pressures of priesthood in Israel at least for a time, but I carried the tears and the prayers of my people with me from Galilee, across the Mediterranean and into Europe.

The combination of prayer, rest, regular meals, and a relatively pressure-free working environment during the summer in Switzerland enabled me to regain my health quickly. I also flourished when regarded and treated as a valued person after so many years of being an unwanted, second-class citizen in Israel. Now in September I had a full schedule of classes.

My involvement in Geneva did not prevent my connection with Ibillin, however. I received many letters as well as daily telephone calls.

"Good morning, Abuna! How are you today?" a cheerful voice would inquire. The people had set up a system whereby someone would go to the next village to use the telephone to greet Abuna. The person would give me the news: "Um Faisal had her baby yesterday, Abuna! Another boy!" "Little Rafi is feeling fine now after his fall from the fig tree!" "Abu Jamal found his donkey, Abuna! It ran off to the other village, can you imagine?" Then the caller would inquire about my health and activities. The appointed messenger went back to Ibillin and told everyone the news about Abuna. How I loved and missed those people and my beloved Galilee!

I once spoke to a group of forty theologians from all over Europe who had come for graduate study in ecumenism at the Institute of Bossey. "One night not too long ago a severe thunderstorm battered my village of Ibillin, and lightning hit the dome of the mosque. The mosque was absolutely unusable, so we invited Abu Muhammad and his Muslim congregation to use the Melkite church for their prayers on Fridays." I could see the sheikh's face very clearly, and I described him to my students. Suddenly I could see many faces of the villagers passing rapidly in front of my eyes. It was very distracting, and I shook my head.

"The Muslim community began praying in the Melkite church," I continued, "and a whole new relationship started to develop in our village. It was a type of . . . of ecumenical . . . relationship."

I could see Sister Gislaine smiling brightly and beckoning me to go visiting homes with her. Mère Macaire offered me a cup of her wonderful tea. Sister Nazarena held a little girl and they both were waving at me. The disconcerting parade of people from Ibillin continued to march in front of my eyes, calling to me: "What are you doing, Abuna? What are you doing in Geneva?"

Turning to the chalkboard, I began writing ideas for ecumenism, trying to ignore the voices that now seemed to shout at me: "Anybody there can give this lecture, but who is going to teach *us*, Abuna? Who is going to talk to us in a simple way and help *us* know these things? Only *you* can do that, Abuna. What are you doing there, Abuna?"

Somehow I muddled through the lecture, very bothered, very confused. Was I going crazy?

After the class I hurried to the chapel and found an isolated corner in which to pray. *God, O God! What is happening to me? Am I sick? Has something snapped in my brain?* I forced myself to be quiet, to let my thoughts focus only on Christ. I thought of his beauty, love, compassion, grace, peace. I pictured myself as a child, roaming the hills near Biram and experiencing the presence of my Champion, the Man from Galilee.

Feeling quieter, I expressed my confusion to God. *I thought I belonged in Geneva, but I am so drawn back to Ibillin, back to Galilee. Am I always to be a refugee, pushed from place to place, never belonging anywhere? Lord, what do you want me to do?*

Soon I knew God's answer. Two weeks later I left Geneva for Israel, filled with ideas and plans. When a community center was built, we could house many more kindergarten children and move the public library out of my bedroom! Maybe we could buy the empty piece of land across from the church! I was jubilant.

However, even as I was traveling to rejoin my beloved community, I was forced to face the reality of our identity and our situation as Palestinians. On September 17, 1970, many Palestinians had been killed by King Hussein's soldiers in Amman, Jordan.[1] The Israelis were battle-ready. I was going home to tension, fear, and possible reprisals.

Nevertheless, I continued to rejoice. I would soon be in Galilee, in Ibillin, with the people whose love was so strong it had reached me in Switzerland. I could almost feel the bishop's hand on my head once again, ordaining me to a dynamic, authentic, and sacrificial priesthood.

Chapter 10

Of Cucumbers, Books, and Pigs

"How many cucumbers have *you* picked, Abuna?"

"Millions of them!" I retorted, tossing one at ten-year-old Butros, who was teasing me from the next row. It was a Sunday afternoon in June 1972.

I was working in the soil of Galilee, in one of Ibillin's distant fields. It was like reliving my childhood in Biram. As a toddler I played on the edge of the field while my family worked. When I was older, I brought water to my parents, but my primary task was to guard our food. In the morning Father dug a shallow hole beside the field, lining it with fig or grape leaves. Our meal, wrapped in a cloth, was placed in the hole, covered with more leaves, and then completely buried. This kept it cool, moist, and fresh, ready for us to eat, a hidden treasure.

One day my parents were harvesting lentils, and I was sitting beside the buried food. "Aren't you tired? Don't you want to eat?" I called.

"No, Son, we must pick the lentils while it is light," Father replied.

The minutes dragged on, feeling like hours, and my stomach hurt. "Is it time to eat yet? Aren't you hungry?" I thought about the tasty bread, the tangy green olives, and the juicy tangerines buried just a meter away from me. *O God*, I prayed, *make them be tired so we can eat.* It finally was too much for a hungry five-year-old boy. I began to cry.

"Elias," Mother called from the field, "if we do not work, I will not find a story about Jesus under the rocks. Let me find a story for you."

76

A story! The thought of Mother's stories immediately stopped my tears. Although Mother could neither read nor write, she had a wonderful memory and a brilliant imagination. She dramatically recited long stanzas of Arabic poems and made Bible stories come alive. The stormy waves splashing against Peter and Andrew's boat in the Sea of Galilee dampened us children, the gritty dust of the Negev Desert blew in our faces as Moses wandered with the Hebrew people, and we gasped when Jesus raised the boy from the dead in the Galilean village of Nain. Listening to stories on Mother's lap, I played with the little brass doves and fish on the long, jingly necklace she always wore, a wedding gift from my father, and I let my imagination roam wherever Mother took me with her words.

"Elias, imagine our Compatriot on the small Mount of Beatitudes, near the Sea of Galilee, talking with the people. He saw they were like a flock of sheep without a shepherd. And he wanted to be their shepherd, Elias."

Suddenly a big, dark mass crashed beside me on a pile of harvested lentils. "Help!" I screamed, frozen in place. "Help me!"

A wounded deer, heavy with milk, had plunged through the fields and collapsed in exhaustion. Quickly Mother dug up our food and gathered our belongings while Father loaded the wounded deer in the basket on one side of our donkey, and me in the other. I rode home patting the beautiful animal, trying to comfort her. My hungry stomach was forgotten.

At home Mother milked the deer to relieve the pressure, and Father poured olive oil on her wounds, explaining that the oil would prevent a big, deadly infection by the flies. Two days later they once again loaded the deer on our donkey, transporting her to the valley below our house. There they freed her, hoping she would soon find her babies.

I continued picking cucumbers with my people until the sun dipped low in the sky.

"It's time to rest and to eat!" Abu Samir called.

Standing up, I stretched my back and legs. Tomorrow I would be aching and stiff, but today I was on the land with my community.

"Come on, Abuna, join us and have some water and fruit," everyone said as I approached the edge of the field and the cool shade under the trees.

"Did you hear about the trouble last night, Abuna?" young Jamal asked. "The police came after midnight and tried to take our neighbor's land."

"When we heard the people's cries, we ran to help," Abu Samir said. "There they were in their nightclothes trying to push the police from their field. The police had already fenced off nearly half the land when they awakened and sounded the alarm. About twenty of us shouted and threatened. Finally the police drove away, leaving the barbed wire behind."

Every summer the Ibillin people who still owned land lived on their distant fields in an effort to prevent confiscation by the Israeli government. Already in 1972 Ibillin had lost thousands of dunums of its best farming land and by the late 1980s would have only a small portion left to cultivate for more than nine thousand inhabitants.[1] This was true not only in Ibillin but also in all the other Galilean Palestinian villages since the establishment of the state of Israel. Some villages like Mi'ilya, a Christian village north of Ibillin, had lost nearly all their land.[2] Government policies appeared to be designed to destroy any sense of permanence Palestinian Israelis might feel and not only to move them from their land and villages but also to remove them altogether from Israel and, after 1967, from the West Bank and the Gaza Strip as well.

From 1948 through the 1950s the land confiscation was easy, because the Palestinians remaining in Israel were frightened, isolated, and without leadership. The best land was taken, declared to be state land, and often annexed to Israeli *kibbutzim*, which could be twenty-five or thirty kilometers away.[3] Once declared to belong to the state, the land was claimed in perpetuity for Jewish people and said to be "redeemed." No matter what the reason or rationale, the end result was the same: Palestinians who hold citizenship in Israel lost and continue to lose their land to government confiscation. They are not allowed to touch the land claimed by the government unless they are hired to work on it.[4]

In 1950, after my father's olive and fig orchards were confiscated in Biram, he and our family agreed to work in our own fields and collect the fruits for the new Jewish owner. Father persuaded us that we, the true owners, would care properly for our beautiful trees and keep them safe and healthy for the next year. Foreigners with no relation to the trees would break the branches, take the fruit, and kill the trees.

Some of our trees were more than a thousand years old. Chacour forefathers had planted them, tended them, and passed them on to us. Other trees in our village were closer to two thousand years old. People in our generation plant trees for their children's children. It was too much to think of these precious trees being neglected or even destroyed by uncaring strangers. After three years, however, Father himself refused to do the work any longer. We were becoming slaves, and our personal dignity, our very soul, was too much to sacrifice. If the trees were destroyed when we returned, Father said, we would plant new ones and begin all over.

In 1951 the Supreme Court of Justice ruled that the people of Biram and Ikrit, another Christian Palestinian village in Galilee that had suffered the same fate, had the right to return.[5] In a countermove, the military authorities in Galilee issued retroactive expulsion notices to the villagers and proclaimed the areas of Biram and Ikrit to be military zones, exempt from the court ruling.[6] Once again the villagers of Biram went to court appealing the declaration, and in January 1952 the Supreme Court of Justice again ruled in our favor.[7]

The Biram council asked the military governor for a date when the villagers could return. Instead, the Biram lands were transferred to the Israel Development Authority, and on September 16–17, 1953, the village was destroyed by the Israeli military. The Biram villagers living in Jish gathered on a nearby hill, weeping as they watched explosives being put in place around their houses. Then Israeli Air Force planes roared over them and began bombing the village.[8] In horror my family saw the houses explode and the trees catch fire. The screaming villagers ran to the edge of Biram and saw that bulldozers were already working to complete the destruction. Soldiers met the people and said, "If you want to return now, you can go. The bulldozers will bury you under the rubble of the houses."

My family came to the Bishop's School in Haifa to tell me the devastating news. Together we wept, holding each other closely, grateful we were all alive but suffering a tremendous loss of identity and hope. I still regard the bombing of Biram as a tragic and satanic act.

Mobile Western people have difficulty comprehending the significance of the land for Palestinians. We belong to the land. We identify with the land, which has been treasured, cultivated, and nurtured by countless generations of ancestors. As a child I joined my family in moving large rocks from the fields. We lay with our backs on the ground and our feet on the rock and pushed, *pushed*, all together. Little by little, "slow by slow," the rock was moved to the side of the field. Perspiration rolled off our bodies, and blood often streamed from our feet, soaking into the ground. It took months to clear the stones from just a small field. The land is so holy, so sacred, to us because we have given it our sweat and blood. It rewards us with wonderful, immense crops. Father could collect up to three tons of dry figs from his fields. Palestinians are at one with their land, and part of them dies when they must be separated from it.

One of the Zionist myths is that Palestine was a wasteland when the state of Israel was established. The Palestinian farming techniques were not modern ones, of course, but they were tailored to the land. Beautiful terracing with hand-built stone walls surrounded the hills, utilizing and protecting the land. The olive, fig, and almond trees were carefully tended, the fields lovingly cultivated.

The wasteland myth is accompanied by the "empty land" myth. Palestine has been depicted as "a land without a people for a people without a land." The empty land myth made the wasteland myth believable. The world has been persuaded by the myths and has not recognized the loss and pain of Palestinians.

"Abuna, what is the news about the community center?" someone asked. "We have been away in the fields for three weeks and have not heard about its progress."

Everyone was delighted when I told them the ground floor was completed and the first-floor concrete had been poured. Then I described the various activities that would take place in the completed building: the kindergarten, meetings, social events, programs, plays, a club for the elderly, and the library.

"This is excellent news for me because I can barely turn around in my bedroom anymore!" I exclaimed. Everyone laughed. They had all visited the library, gone to meetings, and had tea with me in my room and knew how crowded I was. In fact, I now had a new bedroom on the first floor of the parish house, which had been built shortly after I returned from Geneva. The nuns occupied the whole ground floor, and I had three rooms on the first floor. The library was located in all three rooms and was spilling over.

I felt a tug on my sleeve. Turning, I saw Huda. Her black hair nearly covered her bright eyes as she shyly ducked her head. "Huda, my dear, what do you want to say to Abuna?" I gathered the child in my arms and hugged her.

"Abuna," the child whispered, "when are we going to have another Day of the Book?"

"That will come in August. Have you read lots of books, Huda?"

Huda bobbed her head up and down, her eyes still fastened on my face.

"How many books have you read so far?" I asked, leaning close so she could whisper in my ear. When she told me, I was genuinely surprised. "Why, Huda, that's *great!* May I tell the others how many books you have read?"

She nodded, smiling.

"My friends, Huda, who is eight years old and in the third level of the elementary school, has read 127 books since the last Day of the Book!"

The adults gasped and began to applaud the child.

The Ibillin library had become an important part of village life. Zada and other volunteers had worked tirelessly to organize the books and help people use the library. The annual Day of the Book had begun in 1971 when we set aside a whole day to celebrate the reading achievements of people in the village with special honors and recognition.

We were witnessing a genuine cultural revolution in Ibillin. Mothers would say, "And you, my child, how many books did you read this year? Are you going to read more next year? See how many books your cousin has read!" Children and young people were ashamed to walk in the street without a book in their hand.

Not only was this happening in Ibillin but in other villages as well. By raising money in the villages and among friends in Europe, I was able to assist the villages of Mi'ilya and Jish in building community centers of their own. All three of these centers along with projects in other villages were of major importance to the Palestinians in Galilee. There was a sense of bonding, a knowledge they were not alone after all. In fact, constructing a building of any sort and making improvements to existing buildings gave tremendous encouragement to the Palestinian people. It represented permanence and growth as opposed to uprooting and homelessness.

Before leaving my Melkite community in their fields, I prayed with them. During the day I had heard the people singing the songs of the liturgy as they picked cucumbers. They may not have been in the church that morning for the Divine Liturgy but they were praying on their hands and knees in the soil of Galilee, the place in which God chose to live as a human being in the person of Jesus Christ.

🌿

"Abuna!" The deputy mayor of Ibillin, Abu Muhammad, burst into my room. "The police have taken possession of the slaughterhouse!"

"What are you talking about? Where are all the workers?"

"You must come! The Jewish owners of the pig farm came with the police about two hours ago and evicted our men from the slaughterhouse. We tried to get back in, but it's impossible. Please come and help us!"

Quickly the two of us got into my little car and drove the seven kilometers to the confrontation site. Religious Jewish dietary laws forbid the eating of pork, but the Israeli government authorized the raising and slaughtering of pigs in selected areas inhabited primarily by Christian Arabs.[9] One of the biggest pig farms and slaughterhouses in Israel happened to be in my parish, and more than one hundred Christian and Muslim men from the village were employed there.[10] The meat was shipped to Tel Aviv and sold as "steak lavan" or "white steak" to avoid mentioning pork. Harassment from the Jewish pig farm owners and the police was fairly common, but never had the workers been expelled.

Thirty policemen were guarding the entrance gate. The Jewish pig farm owners were inside the slaughterhouse. The workers and many villagers were outside. The mood was extremely tense.

"Abuna, they pushed us out!" one of the workers cried. "They just came in and ordered us to get out, and when we wouldn't move, they forced us to go. They said we can't work here anymore. We depend on that money for our families. Abuna, talk to them. Tell them they have to get out!"

"Please stay back from the gate," I shouted. I didn't want anyone to be near the police or the guns. The people obeyed.

I approached the gate. "I want to speak to the officer in charge," I said in a loud voice.

A stocky man with light blue eyes slowly walked toward me. "Who are you?"

"I am the parish priest in Ibillin."

"What are you doing here? Go back to your church."

"My church is here, with the livelihood of my people." I continued to speak loudly, making sure everyone could hear.

"Whom do you represent?"

Before I could answer, someone from Ibillin shouted, "He represents all of us. Abuna *is* the village, and he speaks for us in one voice." .

The words were an echo from the previous February 22 when I had been honored with Ibillin's First Citizen award. In the presence of my parents and many invited guests, the mayor thanked me for the projects I had initiated in the village and for being a priest to everyone in Ibillin. When the ceremony was at its peak, my mother stood up and, in the Arab fashion, created a song as she sang, improvising the words. The people clapped in rhythm, joining her in a familiar refrain. Mother's song was like a Magnificat, expressing her joy that her son had been awarded the First Citizenship in this faraway village.

Then my mother sang to me. "Do not forget, you are not the first in this village. You must be the last because you are to be the servant, as your Lord Jesus was the servant to all. That is why you became a priest."

Mother's song had been so incredibly beautiful and holy to me that I had wept.

Now I spoke to the police officer in front of the slaughterhouse. "Sir, you had better open this gate now and let me in," I said loudly, "or we will open it by our own means."

The policemen stiffened and reached for their guns. I heard a collective gasp from the people of Ibillin.

"Just what are you going to do, priest?" the officer mocked.

I stared at him and felt my stomach knot tightly. *What a good question,* I thought. *What am I going to do?*

Chapter 11

Marching in Jerusalem

"Just what are you going to do, priest?"
The police officer must have assumed I intended violence when I told him we would open the gate by our own means.

Violence was the farthest thing from my mind. I knew of better kinds of power. Speaking as loudly as I could, I announced my intentions. "I will bring newspaper reporters and notable personalities from all over Israel to this gate. They will be fascinated by the story of Jews confiscating a pig slaughtering house in an Arab village. How interesting for them to see the Israeli police siding with oppressors instead of upholding the laws."

The police officer looked at me as if I were crazy. "Do whatever you want," he muttered.

I then instructed the villagers to stand guard but not to take action until I returned from my home.

Using my newly installed telephone, I called the newspaper editors, who promised they would cover the story. Then I spoke with several ambassadors whose acquaintance I had made while at Hebrew University. They assured me they would investigate the situation immediately.

Next I called a United Nations official in Jerusalem who was my friend. "If Ibillin loses the slaughtering house, it will mean the loss of at least one hundred jobs as well as tax money for the municipality. What these Jewish pig farm owners are doing is absolutely unlawful. Not only is it a violation of civil laws, but it is also against Jewish religious laws and traditions." The U.N. official, like all the others, promised swift investigation.

Next I telephoned the Melkite bishop Joseph Raya. I knew he would be the first to protest this injustice.

As we spoke, I heard a big commotion. "Abuna! Abuna! Come quickly!" people called from the street. I ran out to find many villagers smiling and shaking every hand in sight.

"Don't worry, Abuna!" they shouted. "The police and the Jewish owners all drove away five minutes after you left. We have possession of the slaughterhouse and have left guards. Journalists came to interview us. Do you think this will be in the newspapers?"

I laughed, feeling great relief. As I had hoped, the very idea of publicity throughout Israel had been enough to halt the takeover. "Yes, and that will be our best insurance that this will not happen again, my friends. Today we won a great victory with nonviolent tactics, which, in the long run, are much more effective than violence."

"Well, Abuna Elias," Bishop Raya said a few days later, "you have caused quite a stir among the newspapers, the ambassadors, the U.N., the Orthodox rabbis, and the Israeli general public!"

"Yes, indeed!" I said, not able to keep from laughing. "The rabbis are absolutely appalled and are sparing no words in castigating the owners. Of course, the Orthodox Jews want to eliminate the pig farming operation altogether, but it is far too profitable for that. The owners will keep a low profile from now on, I am sure, and Ibillin will have no more trouble."

"Congratulations, my son! God used your words and actions in a mighty way."

The bishop's warm words and his understanding of our situation were delightful to hear. My relationship with Joseph Raya had been excellent from the first day he became bishop. Although he was Lebanese, Bishop Raya had a keen sensitivity to the Palestinian justice issues. He had lived in the United States and had worked closely with civil rights activist Martin Luther King, Jr.

"That was quite a controversial statement the Committee of Biram made a few weeks ago," the bishop said, grinning as he lit his pipe.

In a time of great despair over the Israeli government's refusal to permit the people from Biram to return, the Committee of Biram had published an open letter. In it they invited the government to send some rabbis to circumcise all males of Biram so they would have the right to return to the village. The Melkite and Maronite Christians would never agree to circumcision, of course, and they knew that no rabbis would agree to perform them, but it was a way of saying, "We know very well that we are not given the right to return because we are not Jews. If becoming Jews will make the difference so we can live in our village and farm our land, then we are willing to do even that."

The Law of Return passed in 1950 gives any Jewish person in the world the gift of immediate citizenship in Israel and the right to live in the land.[1] But the Palestinians from whom the land was taken are not given the right to return to their land and homes. This dark side of Zionism focuses on building a state not *for* the Jews but *of* the Jews, and *only* of the Jews. Other people, particularly the Palestinians, even those with Israeli citizenship, are not considered to have the same rights, especially in relation to the land. Some Zionist extremists declare openly that the Palestinians must be removed altogether from Israel, the West Bank, and Gaza. The Committee of Biram was founded by its residents to try every nonviolent means to gain their return to Biram, but still in 1972 it had been unable to exert enough legal or political pressure on the Israeli government to implement the court's ruling.

Bishop Raya had taken a strong interest in the problems of Biram and Ikrit. Their lands were part of his diocese, and many of the refugees were Melkites. Soon he had learned that one of his priests, Abuna Elias, was from Biram. With his civil rights experience in the United States, the bishop wanted to take action on behalf of the people of the two villages. "What would you think, Abuna Elias, if you and I went to visit Golda Meir?" the bishop had asked one summer day in 1972.

"That sounds excellent! Has she invited us?"

"No, she hasn't," Bishop Raya chuckled, "but what if we made an effort to speak with the prime minister, presenting the case for Biram and Ikrit in a personal, compelling way?"

"My dear bishop, if you go to speak with Golda Meir, I will be right by your side. You could not keep me away!"

On August 8, 1972, Bishop Raya and I had our meeting with Golda Meir.[2] I had seen her picture many times, but I was not prepared for the cold personality we encountered. The prime minister sat woodenly in front of us, seeming almost senseless to what we were saying. Both the bishop and I spoke about the court decisions giving the people of Biram and Ikrit the right to return, pleading with her to let the decision be carried out.

"Impossible. For state reasons we cannot allow them to return," was all Golda Meir would say in response to our request.

"You have criticized the pope for not recognizing Israel and for receiving Yasser Arafat," the bishop said. "But, Madame Golda Meir, if you live in a glass house, you are not permitted to throw stones at your neighbors. You have killed justice in this country because you will not allow the people of Biram and Ikrit to return to their homes.

"Because you have killed justice in Israel, we will declare next Sunday a day of mourning. We will not pray the Sunday prayers nor will we celebrate the Eucharist. We will only toll the church bells as a sign of mourning for the death of justice in Israel."

"Oh, Bishop," I protested, "we do not want Golda Meir to be the Jezebel of the twentieth century. Naboth is still alive."

Naboth, a Gentile, owned a vineyard next to the country palace of King Ahab and Queen Jezebel in the northern kingdom, Israel, in the ninth century B.C. Ahab wanted to purchase the vineyard but Naboth refused, wishing to keep it as a family inheritance. Jezebel proceeded to secure the land for her husband through deceit and gross injustice. Naboth was stoned to death on a false conviction of blasphemy that Jezebel arranged. Jezebel then told Ahab that Naboth was dead and he could take possession of the vineyard. The prophet Elijah found the king in Naboth's vineyard and said, "Have you killed, and also taken possession?" Elijah described how God would punish both Ahab and Jezebel for this evil act.

"Naboth, in the form of the people of Biram and Ikrit, is still alive, but his land has been taken," I said directly to the prime minister. "But it is not too late to correct the injustice. Madame

Prime Minister, you need only to have the courage to say, 'You have the right to return.'"

Once again Golda Meir said only, "For state reasons we cannot allow you to return. It is impossible." Her expression was stonelike.

"Then, Madame Golda Meir, we invite you to mourn the death of justice, killed by your very own hands," Bishop Raya said as we left her office.

"Bishop," I asked as we drove back to Haifa, "how can we theologically justify closing the churches on Sunday?"

"Look, Elias, our good, almighty God asked us to pray, and we love to pray to our God, but over the centuries God must have become accustomed to our babbling and does not pay attention anymore. We shall stop speaking, and then God will be bothered and say, 'What is wrong, children?' Then we can tell the Almighty what we want and need, and the Lord will hear our words."

I laughed, and Bishop Raya laughed, too. But for me it was the best theology, because it was simultaneously so human and so divine.

The following Sunday was a day of mourning for the thirty-three Melkite churches in Galilee. The bells pealed in protest and proclamations of mourning were posted on the closed church doors.[3]

"How are the plans for the march in Jerusalem progressing?" The bishop observed me through his puffs of smoke. "Do you have the permit?"

"Yes, a Jewish friend went with me to Jerusalem to apply for the permit, and it has been granted for August 23. The Committee of Biram is working hard on this massive effort, arranging all the details."

"The committee chairman visited and asked if I would lead the march," the bishop said, examining his pipe, which now had gone out.

"Excellent! You are just the one to lead us in Jerusalem. You have been such a strong supporter of our efforts to return to Biram and Ikrit."

"Hmm," the bishop murmured, relighting his pipe. "Well, Abuna Elias, although I am greatly honored by the invitation I have declined the offer."

"Why?" I asked, astounded. "You have spoken out so often for Biram and Ikrit, yet you refuse to lead our march? This is the most significant thing we have done. Please reconsider."

He shook his head. "No, my son. I have made up my mind. You, Elias Chacour, should lead the march."

I was speechless. Me? Lead the protest march? I shook my head.

"Yes, the committee and I are agreed, Abuna Elias, that you as a Palestinian, as a refugee from Biram, and as a well-known graduate of Hebrew University should be the leader. I am supportive of the cause, but I am Lebanese. I will march with you, but you must be the leader."

Much later I left the bishop, having promised I would lead the march in Jerusalem. It was an honor, yes, but the whole protest was fraught with danger. Never before had the Palestinians inside Israel protested as a group. None of us knew what the outcome might be. We did not want bloodshed, of course, but the possibility it might occur was very great. The Palestinians were going into Jerusalem, into the heart of the Jews, and saying, "We are not happy because you are unjust."

O God, this is so big, I prayed. *The confrontation at the pig slaughterhouse was nothing compared to the march. Protect everyone, Lord—those who march, those who watch and listen, those who agree with our protest, those who disagree. And through it all, may our cries for justice be heard.*

The protest march began at Jaffa Gate in the Old City of Jerusalem on August 23, 1972, and I was amazed to see the thousands of participants. The mix of Jews, Christians, Muslims, and Druze was beautiful. I had invited people from Hebrew University to join us, but I was overwhelmed when at least seventy professors came to manifest their solidarity with me and our cause. Bishop Raya was there, ready to march, speak, and participate.

Busloads of people traveled from Galilee that morning, including my parents. Mother was concerned for my safety, but what mattered to me, first of all, was that the protesters conduct themselves according to the committee's plan, only marching, singing, and carrying their signs, and, second, that everyone— Jews, Muslims, Christians, Druze—*everyone* be protected from any harm. The message we carried was of the utmost importance, but it would get lost if there were violence. And violence would make it nearly impossible to get a hearing on Palestinian issues inside Israel again. The whole idea of a march on behalf of Biram and Ikrit was extremely risky, we knew, but also had the potential to do much good.

Mother and Father could not physically make the march and were settled at a corner where they could watch. As the moment came for the march to begin, I was brought to a jeep that would drive slowly at the front of the procession. I sat on top of the jeep, in as visible a position as possible. Right behind me were people carrying signs declaring the right of the Biram and Ikrit people to return to their homes and land.

Slowly the jeep began to move along Mamilla Road. My heart was pounding as I shouted slogans and led people in singing. We really, truly were doing this, despite all the opposition. Behind me I could see the incredible mix of protesters. Ahead I could see Israeli police and soldiers, weapons at the ready. All around I saw curious onlookers reading our signs and watching the unlikely parade wind through Jerusalem. Many photographers and journalists were at work covering the event.

I saw my parents on their corner. Mother was obviously praying. I could imagine how vulnerable I must appear to them, because I was feeling extremely vulnerable myself. It was thrilling and frightening all at once. *O God, may people see and hear our cause today because of our actions.*

Finally we arrived at the prime minister's office, the end of the march, where speeches were given. Journalists had questions to ask, and I was happy to give the interviews. Later the newspapers gave good coverage to our march, and the news was also carried in foreign papers.[4]

I was grateful there had been no violence, no bloodshed. Palestinians inside Israel had been given the opportunity to speak out, and some Jewish people heard their cries for justice and were willing to support them publicly. The march was effective in telling Israel and the world about Biram and Ikrit, but the Israeli government made no changes in its policies. Golda Meir repeated on the radio what she had previously said to Bishop Raya and me: "For state reasons we will never give them the right to return." She also said that if the government gave the people of Biram and Ikrit the right to return, it would establish an undesirable precedent. No amount of persuasion from the courts or from concerned groups and individuals ever swayed her from that position.

"Elias, there are forces at work to expel me from the position of bishop." Joseph Raya had come to Ibillin to visit privately. "It's no secret the Israeli authorities are very angry about my public support for Palestinian causes. The government hates me and wants me removed."

"That is true, no question about it," I agreed. "You have been wonderfully outspoken." We chuckled together momentarily.

"But that's not all, Elias. I have also spoken out about injustices within our Melkite church. I do not have the support of the patriarch or the majority of the priests in this diocese. There are many undercurrents, and I expect I will soon be dragged out of office."

The political undercurrents were real, and it was sickening to see priests' personal ambitions taking precedence over parishioners' needs, to observe the machinations against this sensitive and caring man.

"Well, if the patriarch wants you out, if priests in the diocese are working against you, and if, the Israeli government wishes to have you removed, you have no hope of staying. The only question is how long your expulsion will take."

"I know. Well, in the meantime, perhaps I can make a difference for people while I still have the authority and opportunity."

"What will you do, if indeed you are removed as bishop?"

"Oh, I will probably go back to Canada or the United States and work on human rights causes there. At least I will be at peace with my conscience. I will be fine. Don't you worry, my friend."

We enjoyed the tea Sister Nazarena brought us. As the afternoon shadows lengthened, we were just two friends who enjoyed each other's company.

The shadows eventually swallowed Joseph Raya. Within a year and a half he was gone. I had lost a valued bishop, supporter, confidant, and friend.

Chapter 12

Welcome to Beirut, Abuna!

"Your new cassock looks very nice, Abuna."

"Thank you, Sister Gislaine. I am leaving for Lebanon right after breakfast. Tomorrow I will visit the patriarch in Beirut. Goodness, the last time I saw him he was still bishop of all Galilee, living in Haifa. That was before I went to Geneva." I brushed an insect off my sleeve. *The new gray cassock* is nice, I thought, *so immaculate.* I had not purchased one in many years.

"Will you see your family in Lebanon, Abuna?"

"Yes, indeed. My uncle and his family still live in Dbayeh refugee camp near Beirut. I will celebrate the liturgy in the camp next Sunday."

We sat down at the breakfast table, and I blessed the food.

"I have heard many ugly stories about shootings and kidnappings in Lebanon," Sister Gislaine said. "Is it safe to travel there?"

"Now you are sounding like Mère Macaire, God rest her soul." The elderly nun had recently died in the convent in Nazareth. "I have my Israeli passport, an exit visa from Israel, an entrance visa to Lebanon, and a *laissez passer* from the Vatican. I will be fine."

"How are plans progressing for the summer camp, Abuna?" Sister Nazarena asked.

"Very well. The committee met last night, and the 1975 Summer Camp of the Book will serve more than two thousand children from fifteen villages."

In 1973 I had initiated the camp program, expecting five hundred children. More than eleven hundred came. For three weeks, instead of playing in the hot streets, the children camped under the olive trees around Ibillin, playing and learning together, visiting the holy places and each other's villages, and reading books at least one hour daily. Each summer we hoped to have Jewish children join us, but it was impossible. Instead, we were happy to welcome Jewish volunteer workers.

To the children gathered under the olive trees I would say, "Remember, your roots in Galilee go back long before the two-thousand-year-old trees. Your Palestinian ancestors planted these trees, and loved the land. It is from this land you have been removed and to this land you will someday return. From this land God took human form. In this land Jesus of Nazareth gave his blood for the redemption of the world. Perhaps you will have to do something with your blood to redeem Jews and Palestinians and to create an environment of negotiation, love, and tolerance."

An hour later I crossed the border into Lebanon and took a taxi to Sidon, where I boarded a collective taxi with six other persons for the trip to Beirut. I was enjoying seeing the Lebanese people, villages, and scenery once again, but the tense political atmosphere in April 1975 could be felt even in the taxi. No one was willing to trust a stranger, it seemed, not even when that stranger was a priest. Any conversation was limited to the only safe subject, the weather.

The silence allowed me to think about my sermon. Jesus and his disciples encountered a blind man in Jerusalem. The disciples asked, "Teacher, who sinned, this man or his parents, that he was born blind?" What could I say about this scripture to my people who had been refugees in Lebanon for twenty-seven years? Who had sinned, the refugees or their families, that they had to endure exile, pain, and suffering? This sermon was not going to be easy.

In less than an hour we were on the outskirts of Beirut. We stopped briefly while a passenger made a telephone call, then continued into the city. *Soon I will see my uncle for the first time in many years,* I thought.

We had driven only a short way when two dusty, nondescript cars suddenly surrounded the taxi. The right back door was jerked open by a soldier. He looked quickly at the passengers and then pointed at me.

"You! Get out!" he demanded.

"Who are you?" Fear flooded my body and I felt paralyzed.

"It's not your business. Get out!"

Still I did not move.

The driver, apparently a Christian, turned and spoke urgently to me. "Abuna, get out if you want to save your life." In his eyes I could see a silent plea for his own safety and that of the other passengers.

I forced myself out of the car. Now I could see there were six men dressed in green fatigues with *keffiyehs* around their heads and necks, pointing guns at me. *Goodness,* I thought, *one man and one gun would have been enough to handle this priest.*

A soldier took my arm and dragged me away from the taxi.

"I want to take my bags," I shouted, remembering my Bible, liturgical books, and the gifts for my family. Wrenching myself free, I tried to reach my luggage.

"No, leave it!" the soldier yelled.

I planted my feet and folded my arms across my chest, taking a stubborn stance. "No, I *won't* leave it! Kill me right here if you want, but I will not leave without my luggage."

The soldier glared at me. I glared back.

"Take it, then," he muttered.

Quickly I opened the trunk, grabbing my two bags, which in turn were grabbed from me. While being roughly pushed into the nearest vehicle, I heard a voice from the taxi say, "Well, this man will be killed now." No one had moved to help me.

Two soldiers jumped into the backseat on either side of me, their guns on their laps. The driver sped away, the tires screaming. The second car followed as we continued on the road into Beirut.

I looked at my captors. We were sitting shoulder to shoulder, and they both were staring straight ahead, tough and determined.

"Who *are* you?" I demanded. I could not tell if they were Lebanese, Palestinian, or Syrian, or whether they were official or self-appointed soldiers. Knowing who had kidnapped me was crucial for survival.

"It's not your business," my initial captor said, not looking at me.

"I need to know," I insisted. "Who are you?"

The other man snarled, "If you want to stay alive, you better shut up." He jerked his gun toward me for punctuation.

"Well, if you are official soldiers, I am not afraid of you," I said, trying to change the atmosphere. "You cannot be bad." But after that the men would not speak to me at all. I prayed and prayed to God, who was also being very silent. *Why have they kidnapped* me? *I have no political connections, I have no money. O God, O God.*

After driving perhaps thirty minutes, we turned onto a narrow, dusty path. Very soon we drove into a jungle of spiny cactus trees, so thick the car could barely pass through.

Entering a walled village, we were surrounded by tiny buildings jammed together. Slowly we drove through a maze of narrow streets, winding left, right, left. I quickly lost my bearings. Now I knew why I had not been blindfolded. Never could I find my way back to this place, and, besides, they must intend to kill me.

Finally we stopped deep within the village. I was hauled up a flight of steps in a corner building and pushed into a small room. The men locked the door and disappeared.

"Where is my luggage?" I shouted. No one answered.

A table and three straight-backed chairs were the only furnishings. The one window was tightly boarded. A single bulb hung from the ceiling. *Is this someone's home, or place of business?* Long minutes passed. *God, give me the words to say, the strength to endure whatever is coming.*

The door opened. Four men entered, carrying guns. The leader, perhaps thirty years old, his *keffiyeh* loosely draped around his shoulders, sat in a chair behind the table, ordering me to sit in front of him. He stared at me. I stared back. Was he Lebanese? Palestinian? Syrian? Or perhaps Jewish Israeli dressed as an Arab? It was impossible to tell.

"Who are you?" he asked in Arabic.

"I am Abuna Elias Chacour."

"Where are you coming from?"

"From Israel."

"Where is that, Israel?" I knew immediately I had made a mistake.

"Sorry. From Occupied Palestine." *My first clue,* I thought. Either this was an Israeli playing a game with me, or it was an Arab who rejected the reality of the state of Israel. More likely the latter.

The leader looked carefully at my face, at my clothing, at my shoes, and back at my face. "How did you come to Lebanon?"

"I came officially over the border at Rosh Hanikra, and I have my permits." I gave him the Vatican *laissez passer.*

He tossed it back. "No, not this. Give me your papers."

I could see malevolence and scorn cross the man's face when he examined my Israeli passport. My heart sank to my shoes. *How can I explain to this man that I am an Arab Palestinian with Israeli papers? How can I tell him I am not his enemy, despite my identity as an Israeli? How insane my life is,* I thought. *The Jewish Israelis see me as an Arab and an enemy despite my papers. Arabs see me as an Israeli and an enemy because of my papers. No wonder we Palestinians inside Israel hardly know who we are anymore.* More immediately, however, I knew I was in serious trouble. I could be killed instantly in this hidden place, and only God would ever know.

"Where were you born?" the leader asked, studying my documents.

"I was born in Biram."

"Biram. Where is that?"

"In Upper Galilee. Goodness, you do not know the problems of Biram and Ikrit and how we are fighting against the Jews to return home?"

The leader frowned, narrowing his eyes as he looked at me. "Fighting against the Jews? Aren't you a Jew?"

Ah, my second clue. Despite my priest clothing, they think I am Jewish. No wonder I am seen as a threat. "No, of course not. I am a Christian. I am a Palestinian."

"Palestinian. Biram." He tapped his fingers on the table. "Prove to me that you have been fighting for your rights to return."

Clue number three! These were Palestinians! Now I knew what to say and how to say it! In elaborate detail I described the various protests the Committee of Biram had conducted, including the massive march into Jerusalem. "I have come to visit relatives in Dbayeh camp and will celebrate the liturgy with them on Sunday. I truly am a Christian, a Palestinian, and a priest," I said, pointing at my cassock, which by this time was dusty and rumpled.

Slowly the leader came around the table and nodded at his men. *God, is this it? Have I completely misread this man, this whole situation?* I could not breathe, fully expecting a bullet in my brain or my heart, yet somehow it seemed I was above the scene, watching my own execution.

The leader continued to study me, then smiled broadly, grasping my shoulders and pulling me to my feet. "Abuna Elias Chacour, I hope you understand why we kidnapped you."

I began to breathe heavily. Relief infused every part of my body. The leader pulled a chair in front of mine, and we sat facing each other. Someone opened the door, and cool air gusted up the stairs, carrying children's laughter and a *muezzin's* call to prayer from the mosque.

"We are Abu Amar's people." Yasser Arafat, chairman of the executive committee of the Palestine Liberation Organization (PLO), is often called Abu Amar by his friends and followers. The nickname means "Father of the Structure, or Building."

"You are in Sabra refugee camp in Beirut," the leader said. "We have information that three hundred foreigners are infiltrating into Lebanon, pushed by the Zionists and the Americans, to burn as many churches and mosques as possible. That, of course, would set the religious populations against each other and cause incredible fear, hatred, and reprisals. The Palestinians will be blamed. More of us will die, many will suffer. We must police Lebanon so the infiltrators cannot do their work."

This was actually beginning to make sense. "And you thought I was one of those infiltrators. But why me? I am a priest."

"We received a tip that a Jewish man dressed like a priest, traveling with an Israeli passport, crossed the border this morning. Disguised as a priest, he would have easy access to any church. Our tip said this priest was obviously wearing a brand new robe and seemed uncomfortable in it."

I was aghast. *My new cassock—and the fact I am not yet accustomed to it?* I began to laugh. *This is too wild, too incredible!* All the men laughed with me and pointed at my cassock.

As the laughter subsided, the leader spoke quietly. "Abuna, my village in Palestine was destroyed in 1947." Soon I determined his home village was Saffuri, formerly located very near Ibillin. I knew many people from Saffuri and began to name them, describing how they looked, the condition of their health, how many children they had, and where they were now living.

The man was very moved and asked many questions. Finally he stood and drew me to my feet, shaking my hand. "Abuna Chacour, I apologize for kidnapping you. Now you can consider yourself to be our commander. Whatever you want us to do for you, we are ready."

Soon I and my luggage were transported to a church where my relatives awaited me. I felt disoriented, confused. Had all this really happened to me? Was it some weird nightmare? But no, it was painfully real, and I knew how simple and easy it would have been to kill me. A few years later I was terribly saddened to learn that everything the men in Sabra camp had told me that day proved to be absolutely true.

The next day I visited with the patriarch of the Melkite church, my old friend, George Hakim. We reminisced about the ordination service in 1965, and I felt very close to the patriarch. When invited, I spoke honestly and confidentially about my concerns and fears regarding the appointment of the next bishop in our diocese, now that Bishop Raya was gone.

The celebration of the Divine Liturgy in Dbayeh camp was extremely emotional for me, communing with the Christians living in such poverty and under such duress. Not only had they lost their lands and homes in Palestine, but they also were unwelcome in Lebanon. Now in 1975 the various political factions were all struggling for power. War seemed inevitable. The Palestinians knew they were in a very dangerous position.

Looking out on the congregation, I could see twelve-year-old Amira, the beautiful daughter of my uncle, Hanna. Her eyes were shining in joy as she prayed with her cousin, Abuna Elias. That was a picture of her I would always remember.

More than twenty tape recorders were arranged around the altar, and I knew many groups of people would eventually hear me speak. My words needed to be measured carefully, but I was committed to preach the truth. "Who has sinned, the Palestinians or their ancestors, to have to endure such suffering and such pain? To lose their homes, their lands, their dignity, their future, their dreams? To have to live in a foreign land, unwelcome and persecuted, sometimes even to die? Who has sinned?

"Or is our suffering, like that of the blind man, intended to show God's love and glory to others, to the world? It would be easy to focus on our pain and on our loss, using this exile as a time of bitterness, hatred, and revenge. But with hope and faith in God and the love of God through our Savior Jesus Christ, we know we can never be destroyed by the powers of sin and evil. We call upon God to release us from our suffering, to work a mighty work in us so that God may be glorified. We must plead with God to keep us from ever causing anyone to become a refugee because of us. Despite our suffering, loss, and pain, we can be renewed in the hope and faith that God can and will work a miracle in and through us, thereby manifesting God's power and glory for all to see."

I embraced everyone. Through our tears we promised to pray for one another. Amira stayed right beside me until it was time to leave.

Two days later I was in Ibillin, rejoicing that I could live in Galilee and vowing to tell the Palestinian story to the world. I savored the hot tea Sister Gislaine had poured for me as I listened to her news. The Melkites had heard the patriarch was about to name the new bishop. There was much speculation about the rumored choice, a priest from Lebanon who was presently serving a small parish in Upper Galilee.

"How was your trip, Abuna?" Sister Nazarena inquired, bringing a bowl of fruit to the table. "Did anything exciting happen?"

I almost choked, spattering some tea on the front of my cassock.

Sister Gislaine ran for a damp towel and sponged off the tea stains. "There, Abuna, it's fine now. It would be a shame to spot your brand new cassock while it still looks so beautiful. Did you enjoy wearing it on your trip to Beirut?"

Chapter 13

This Man Is Like Ashes

Village life in Biram was simple, but such simplicity did not mean isolation, ignorance, or a disinterest in education. Father often went to Haifa for trade or medical purposes, either by foot or on his donkey, a three- or four-day trip. The villagers journeyed to Damascus, Beirut, or Jerusalem, but never thought of going to live in Lebanon, for instance. Their Galilee was beautiful, their lands fertile. Why go elsewhere?

Sometimes I would peek in the door of the mayor's house to see the battery-powered radio. The mayor and the other elders would listen to the news and tell the villagers. Big-city newspapers were shared. The neighboring Jewish village with which we traded was another source of news. When I was young, I learned that terrible things were happening to our Jewish "cousins," as we called them, all of us being Semitic people. "The Jews are being persecuted and killed in Europe by a devil named Hitler," Father told us, and we often prayed for them.

As a family we knelt to pray each day around the fire in the corner of our house. Being a lively child, I would sometimes jump and play while the others prayed, but I heard Father improvise prayers for his children, church, fields, orchards, and for peace in the land. Many times I heard him pray, "Lord, do not forget to liberate the persecuted Jews from the hand of the cruel Hitler." We never imagined that in a few years Jewish Zionist soldiers would trick us into leaving our village and take our lands, using Hitler's persecutions as one of the reasons they, not we Palestinians who had lived here for so many centuries, should have the land.

103

All I could understand at the age of eight was that everyone I loved was frightened, miserable. Our beautiful world of village life was destroyed. Our dreams and expectations for the future in Biram had vanished.

I loved going to school in Biram and learning from my teachers, the village priests. Father was personally determined that his own children would be well educated. As the oldest son, Father had attended school for only five years before leaving to help his brother and sister become educated. Father, however, was able to read and write better than many today who have finished secondary school. He instilled in us a great ambition to learn.

Father knew the priests were the best-educated people in the village and resolved that one of his sons would become a priest. Rudah was sent to Nazareth to study in the seminary preparatory school, but he stayed only a short while. Chacour refused to go at all.

Mousa and Atallah were sent together to prepare for the priesthood, but that ended disastrously in 1947. Atallah returned home frightened because Mousa, about fourteen years old, had run away. Father, Rudah, and Chacour hunted for him, but Mother blamed Father for the situation: "You want them to become priests in spite of their will. Now you have lost Mousa forever."

After three months one of the village men came rushing to tell us that a visitor from Jordan had spoken about a boy who had run away from Galilee and was now perhaps in Zarqa, a town just north and east of Amman.

Riding his donkey, Father traveled south by the Sea of Galilee and crossed the Jordan River at a shallow point. In the Zarqa area he found Mousa as well as Chacour relatives. Overjoyed to see Father, Mousa was anxious to return home if he didn't have to be a priest. Father agreed, and they traveled back to Biram. There was great rejoicing in the village with food, music, and dancing because the lost son had been found.

After that, Father did not speak of his sons becoming priests. The seed, however, had been planted in my small head, and even before we were forced to leave Biram and go to Jish, I was thinking about the priesthood. I loved my priest teachers very much. I loved to be in the church and hear all the singing and prayers. And I loved to hear the stories Mother told about Jesus, stories that I sometimes think she gave me with her milk.

While I admired the village priests, it truly was my parents who made Christ real to me. They helped me see Jesus of Galilee as my Champion, my Friend, and my Compatriot, someone to whom I could talk at any time about anything. The courage, sanctity, and simplicity of faith that Mother and Father lived out every day was a powerful example to me.

Our world was infinitely different in Jish from what it had been in Biram. Instead of our comfortable house, all of us were living in one room and grateful to have it. Many of the men of Jish had disappeared, leaving women, children, and older people on their own. Somehow the refugees from Biram were able to fit into what was left of village life in Jish. Eventually there was a makeshift school for the children to attend. I liked it but often longed for my own school and my own priest teachers in Biram.

One day I had a great shock. While playing with other children in a field right by Jish, I noticed a strange stick poking out of the ground. As I jerked on the stick, displacing sand and dirt, I suddenly saw with sickening horror that I was pulling on a human hand. The "stick" was a bony finger, and the flesh had decomposed. When I screamed for my friends, they came running, and we uncovered a man's body, identifiable only because of the clothing. The mystery of what had happened to the men of Jish was solved when our fathers and brothers dug many bodies out of the common grave. They had all been shot. Our family held each other very close that night, mourning the men of Jish and thanking God that the soldiers in Biram had only shot over the heads of our men.

In 1951 the Melkite archbishop of all Galilee, George Hakim, came to visit Jish. The men of the village sat with the bishop, talking, eating, and smoking. He listened to the many stories the men had to tell about Biram and Jish, about the people who had been killed, and about their hardships as Palestinians living in the new state of Israel. The litany of pain and complaints was lengthy.

Finally my father, who had been silent through the whole discussion, began to speak. "Bishop Hakim, I still have one young boy. I want him to become a priest and to study under your guidance. Can you help me?"

The other men were outraged. How dare Abu Rudah ask about his son becoming a priest when there were so many other important problems to solve!

"All right, Abu Rudah," the bishop said, quieting the men. "I will eat with you today, and we will discuss the matter." Later he agreed to take Abu Rudah's youngest son to Haifa and begin his schooling for the priesthood.

I was not consulted about the matter. I was bought and sold at the age of eleven without my knowledge or consent, but despite my fear and pain, I was excited about going to school. Father said there were many books at the Bishop's School in Haifa, and I longed to read them all.

In my growing-up years I had spent many hours roaming in the Galilee hills, talking to my Champion. There was so much I could not understand about my life and about life in general. I told my Friend everything, asked him every question. There were times when I could imagine Jesus striding toward me, smiling, his arms wide open. To me Jesus Christ was very real. Now I needed to leave the hills where I was sure Jesus had run when he was a boy, the hills where he must have walked with his disciples. How would I manage without this land, without my family?

Finally I was at peace. I knew without a doubt that my Friend would be with me in Haifa. In some precious, unexplainable, yet real way, I knew that my Lord Jesus Christ wanted me, Elias, the youngest son of Mikhail, to sacrifice many things and to be a priest.

Picking up the letter from my desk, I read it once again. The statements were absolutely incredible to me. His Beatitude, the patriarch of the Melkite church, George Hakim, had selected a new bishop for the diocese of Akko, Nazareth, Haifa, and all Galilee in this spring of 1975. The patriarch had appointed the very man I had advised him *not* to appoint.

My advice on the matter had been requested secretly in a letter following Bishop Raya's departure in 1974. The patriarch, whom I had known since I was a child, who had ordained me and sent me to Ibillin, who had listened when I challenged him to be a servant—this priest friend had written to ask my opinions about priests whom he was considering to be the bishop. After praying and giving the matter much thought, I wrote my answer. While I had varying opinions about the other candidates, I stated plainly that I was completely opposed to the appointment of a particular Lebanese priest.

This priest had been in a small parish on the Lebanese border in northern Galilee for almost twenty years and seemed merely to exist. In the years I had known him I had not seen a glimmer of spirituality. I wrote these observations to the patriarch and then commented:

> This man has nothing to say to his people. You, Patriarch, might want to light a fire in Israel among the Christians to be more fervent, more active, more dynamic, but this man is like ashes. He cannot light a fire. You can throw some burning charcoal in the ashes and the ashes will become warm, but soon they will extinguish the charcoal, destroying the fire. It will be a catastrophe if you appoint this man as a bishop. He is not fit for that. Anyone else, Patriarch, but not this one.

Finally, I warned the patriarch, "This priest has proved for twenty years that the money he receives from people in this diocese is apparently not spent in the diocese."

My brutal honesty and implicit trust proved to be costly mistakes. A few weeks after the new bishop began his work, I learned that the patriarch had given him my letter. I felt betrayed and extremely vulnerable. A bishop in the Melkite church is answerable only to the patriarch and to God. He has absolute control over the priests and parishes in his diocese, including the priests' salaries and their movement from parish to parish. The appointment as bishop is made for the man's lifetime, however long that may be. All in all, it is a very serious matter for a priest to be at odds with his bishop. After spending much time in prayer, I decided to go to the bishop and face the whole ugly situation head on.

"Bishop, I believe you know that I was consulted and did not agree with your appointment," I said. "I understand you now have a confidential letter I wrote to the patriarch about this matter."

The bishop inclined his head slightly in assent. He was rotund with a round, fleshy face and thinning hair. Light-colored eyes regarded me carefully.

"Despite the things I have written, Bishop, I have come to say that I am ready to do everything possible to help you. I am ready to give you all that God has given me so you can succeed in your tasks and privileges as the bishop of all Galilee, provided you truly work for the diocese."

I did what I needed to do, I thought as I left the bishop. The issue had now been addressed and I was able to express my one condition: "provided you truly work for the diocese." I intended to be watching our new bishop very carefully. In the meantime, I had promised God I would be an obedient priest, submitting to the authority of the bishop.

What an excellent day! On this Friday night in late June 1975 I was tired but very happy. With a busload of people from Ibillin I had visited Mount Hermon and found some snow to throw at everybody. Some of them had never seen or touched snow before.

We ate our picnic lunch at Tel Dan, a lush, green area by the headwaters of the Jordan River. After we hiked to a spot where a spring gushes out of the ground, I spoke about the Lord Jesus as the living water and how we had been immersed in this water at baptism. Then, with my walking stick, I began to splash water on all of them, and they forgot about their problems. They even forgot they were old and became very young again, dragging each other into the water, laughing and playing like children.

Since 1967 I had taken hundreds of busloads of Christian, Muslim, and Druze villagers to Mount Hermon, Tel Dan, the Sea of Galilee, Mount Tabor, and even to my destroyed village of Biram. Sometimes when we stopped to eat, the forty or fifty people would form a circle and do Arabic dances while they sang. They insisted Abuna must dance with them, and I would drag the nuns into the circle, too. The stories flew through the village when we returned: "Abuna danced with us! The nuns danced, too! It was great!"

When we drove back to Ibillin in the evening with everyone so tired and happy, I would talk to them over the microphone on the bus. "Do you realize that our life is like a journey? We have to make it as nice as this day trip has been. Sometimes you were cold and wet today, and I know you are tired now, but it was beautiful because we were all together. Let us make the life in Ibillin as beautiful as this trip."

Now, sitting at my desk after dinner, I heard footsteps entering the large first-floor room. Out of the shadows a familiar figure emerged.

"Good evening, Abuna."

"Good evening, my dear Responsible." I stood up to welcome the man who was still a genius in creating difficulties and obstacles. He was extremely distraught. "Whatever is the matter, my friend?"

"Abuna, my son is lost. He's someplace in Italy, I don't know where. I don't know what to do." Tears spilled over and flowed down his face.

Suddenly I saw my father. He had wept as many tears when Mousa was lost. "Tell me what you know," I said.

The Responsible's son, aged nineteen, was studying medicine in Italy but apparently had had a nervous breakdown. I flew to Italy and found the young man in a hospital. He did not want to return home, believing he had failed his family. Finally, however, he agreed to return, and a genuine reunion and renewal took place. Eventually the young man married and had children. The incident marked a change in the Responsible's attitude toward me. He never fought me publicly again, probably because he knew the other villagers would severely criticize him, saying, "This is not the reward you should give to Abuna, who brought your child alive from the dead."

"Faraj, what are you talking about? This can't be true." I had driven to Rama to see my good friend and was met with dreadful news.

"Elias, calm down. I have accepted it and so must you."
Faraj gave me one of his wonderful smiles, but the fact remained
that my classmate from the Bishop's School in Haifa and the
seminary in Paris, my fellow priest, had multiple sclerosis.

"Are you sure you have seen enough doctors, Faraj? Maybe
there's something new you have missed." I was grasping for any
hope, any comfort.

"Enough, Elias. I have gone to Egypt, to Europe, even to
the United States. I have M.S. and that's it. I have been getting
tired and weak for a long time, and little by little I will lose
control of all my muscles. Already this one leg is almost useless.
I am starting to lose strength in this hand, too. My only prayer is
that I can continue to be a priest."

I held Faraj closely, and we wept together. I wanted to make
everything perfect for him, but it was impossible. Then we
prayed, asking for healing, yes, but asking especially for the
strength to live victoriously with whatever might lie before us.

Chapter 14

We Are Human Beings, Not Cattle or Insects

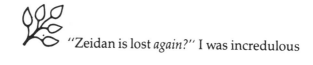

"Zeidan is lost *again?*" I was incredulous and angry.

Just a few months earlier I had brought the young man back from Italy after he, like the Responsible's son, had failed in his studies to be a doctor. Not giving up their dreams of having a doctor son, however, Zeidan's parents had sent him to Clemson University in South Carolina. Now in early 1978 Zeidan had once again disappeared.

"For many weeks we have heard nothing," Abu Zeidan said, barely looking at me. "The university says he left for Israel a month ago. Please, Abuna, can you find Zeidan?" Um Zeidan wept pitifully.

After the family purchased my ticket, I flew to the United States and went directly to Clemson, speaking with university officials and the police. We finally traced Zeidan to an Atlanta hospital. I was taken to a darkened room in the psychiatric unit where Zeidan was curled up on the bed. The police had brought the unidentified, mentally disturbed man to the hospital three weeks earlier.

"Zeidan, I am Abuna Elias Chacour. I have come to take you home." After I repeated this many times, Zeidan slowly turned toward me.

"No, you are not Abuna Elias Chacour. Abuna is in Ibillin."

"Look, Zeidan, here is my passport. Read it." He threw it back.

"No, it is not written Abuna Elias. It's written Elias Chacour. There's no Abuna. You are not Abuna. You are just taking me out to kill me." He turned away, facing the wall.

I knew that Zeidan loved a young woman in Ibillin. I continually spoke her name, saying she was waiting for him. After a long while he responded and eventually agreed to return home, but Zeidan had no clothing and no suitcases. All had apparently been lost at the Atlanta airport when, instead of changing planes to go to New York, he left his luggage in the airport and went outside, becoming completely lost.

Finally, despite great complications, I was able to bring Zeidan to his parents. When Um Zeidan saw her son, she collapsed entirely. He was barely recognizable. Later Zeidan tried to kill himself and his family by burning down the house. Everyone survived, but he made his parents' life a living hell. Um Zeidan cursed me because I had brought the boy back alive.

"Habib, these grapes are going to the summer camps," I said. "Imagine! Nearly four thousand youngsters are going to taste grapes from your vine!"

"I may have given you the vine, Abuna, but it must be the baptism you administered that accounts for such an abundance of fruit each year!" Habib replied.

Habib and I were cutting the big, juicy bunches of purple grapes. The vine not only had spread over the arbor but also had wound its way entirely around the parish house, giving the nuns shade in the hot Galilee summer.

"I heard you had a bad experience in the camp yesterday, Abuna."

"Oooah, Habib! It was downright devilish, and so frightening." My skin crawled at the memory. More than a thousand children were camped near Ibillin in the olive grove near the main road with their counselors, tents, food, and the temporary library. It was one of four summer camp locations in August 1978. About thirty armed Israeli soldiers arrived at noon and asked to inspect the campsite. They found children playing games and reading. Then the soldiers positioned themselves all around the olive grove, watching us. The children remained in their tents.

When the soldiers left, the children ran to see their friends and teachers, reexploring the olive grove. Soon I heard shouts of discovery. "Look what we found!"

We hurried to the place where two boys had discovered a strange object. "What is it, Abuna? It wasn't here before!" Other shouts indicated that more of the strange objects had been found.

I suddenly tasted great fear. God! Were these bombs?

"Get away! Stay out!" I shouted. The counselors quickly took the children to the edge of the olive grove. I ran from one spot to the other, checking the strange little boxes. They had not been here before the soldiers came, that I knew for sure. Could the soldiers possibly have planted bombs in the children's camp? It was too ghastly to contemplate, but the strange objects were in place, and I had a thousand children to think about. I hurried to the nearby gas station and called the police.

"Come quickly! Some terrorist actions are going on here!"

The police were amazed to discover Palestinian children. They had assumed they would find Palestinian terrorists. I explained about the presence of the Israeli soldiers as I pointed out the objects. The police carefully removed them and drove away, leaving us with many questions.

"Habib, I become weak and sick when I think how many children might have been killed," I said. "What kind of demented minds would think of putting bombs in a children's camp? Even if they were not bombs, we were obviously meant to think they were. That's criminal! And absolutely inhuman!"

"It is yet another way of telling us to get out of this land, Abuna. They are saying, 'You are not wanted here and we will do anything to get you out.'"

"Why can't Jewish people understand that we Palestinians love this land and are part of it? We are not cattle or insects to be chased away, but human beings who want to stay in our beloved land. If the Jews want to be here, too, that's fine, but why can't we live together as equals?"

Habib shook his head. There was no answer. We sat together in silence, eating the grapes.

"I have been going to Jish, helping the people enlarge and remodel their community center into a secondary school," I finally said. "Perhaps we here in Ibillin should also be making

113

plans to build a secondary school. It would help our children and village but perhaps it could also serve many other villages in Galilee. What do you think about that?" This was the first time I had mentioned my idea to anyone.

Interest, doubt, curiosity, and then delight were evident in Habib's expression. "Well, well. What an interesting possibility."

"Children of Biram," I shouted, "are you ready to bring life and peace to your village?"

"We're ready! Let's go!" Three hundred and fifty young people, each carrying an olive tree sapling, a bottle of water, and a lunch, cheered when I started leading them along the main road from Jish to Biram.

It was Saturday, February 17, 1979. The Committee of Biram was using the occasion of Israel's annual Day of the Tree to remind Israelis and the world community of our desire to return to Biram and of the court orders affirming our right. Young people from Biram families and Jewish Israeli supporters of our cause had been invited to join the march, bringing olive tree saplings to plant in the destroyed village. The committee had also invited Israel's prime minister, Knesset members, the Israeli police and border police, as well as the national and international press to join us.

None of our special guests arrived, not even news reporters. *Never mind*, I thought. *We will have a wonderful walk in the Galilee sunshine, plant these precious trees in Biram, and let the children play.*

As we walked, I chatted and sang with the children. Being with them in the Galilee hills brought back a flood of memories. Suddenly I was a child again, running with my friends in and around the village, making up our own games.

In the springtime, when the ground was still humid and soft, we sharpened little sticks and threw them at a target. The winners collected all the sticks they knocked down. Sometimes I would have hundreds of these sticks, and would take them home to Mother. She used them for her cooking fire.

114

We caught birds by spreading sticky green glue on big sticks, putting them in the trees. As many as one or two hundred birds might be caught in a day, and each child took some home to eat. They were delicious, especially in August during fig season. The birds ate figs until they were very fat, just right for dinner.

Sometimes we went down into the valley and went fishing in the stream. Water backed up behind big rocks, forming little pools, and we could catch fish with our hands. We put the small fish in water and carried them home, throwing them in our water cisterns to grow. They ate the insects and grew big very quickly. Soon we had a lovely fish dinner.

I loved the poetry competitions to find out who knew the most poems. Perhaps Atallah would start by reciting a poem that ended with the letter *r*, and then Daoud would have to recite a poem that began with the letter *r*. His poem might end with *m*. Then I would have to say a poem starting with *m*, and on we would go for hours. We had to know hundreds and even thousands of poems to select the right one at the right moment.

"Abuna, how much longer before we get to Biram?" Leila asked, tugging at my hand.

"It's not far now," I told the child. Again we sang, this time a part of the glorious Easter liturgy. The parade of olive trees accompanied by its own music threaded its way through the green hills.

Then, as we came around a corner, I saw a crowd of people waiting for us, many of them carrying guns. Rolls of barbed wire blocked our path. I held up my hand, halting the march. Turning to the bewildered children, I told them to stay right where they were.

I walked toward the barbed wire and the many Israeli soldiers and policemen who were gathered on both sides of the blockade. As I approached the officer in charge, news reporters and people with television cameras jockeyed for position. *Goodness*, I thought, *I hope they are getting many pictures of the soldiers and their submachine guns facing the threatening children, the menacing olive saplings, and the dangerous priest.*

"What is wrong, sir?" I asked. "My group of children and I wish to go to Biram."

"No, that is not possible." The officer stood squarely in my path.

"And why not? We pose no threat. We carry only olive saplings."

"We have orders to forbid you entrance to Biram. You must go back."

"No, sir. We want to plant olive trees, symbols of peace." It was a face-off between me and the officer, standing toe to toe, exchanging words, while other soldiers and the photographers encircled us. *O God, keep the children back. They'll be safe if they just stay where I left them.*

"You cannot pass," the soldier said. "That is it. Turn around and no one will be hurt."

"No one will be hurt if you allow us to plant olive saplings on the houses of our fathers and forefathers. Surely that isn't too much to ask, especially when we have just observed the Day of the Tree."

"We have received orders from above. You are forbidden to enter the village of Biram."

I glanced behind me. The children were being very obedient, standing in place. Now they were smiling and holding their olive saplings high for all to see. I began to address the group gathered around the barbed wire, speaking in Hebrew. All Arab Palestinians in Israel understand Hebrew, but most Jews do not understand Arabic.

"Your 'orders from above' are very low orders because they have no morality about them. My dear friends, we love you and regret that you hold those machine guns made to threaten, scare, and kill. When you face olive saplings with machine guns, you have no hope for life. You are scared and you scare others. See these Palestinian youngsters· who are all carrying an olive sapling, the tree of peace that promises to endure for centuries! The children are relaxed while you are very tense with machine guns. We shall never give up, but we shall never carry weapons to plant an olive tree and obtain our human rights to home and freedom."

While the cameras kept rolling, I walked back to the young people. "Children of Biram, we are turning around. We'll plant the trees another day." I began singing our Easter liturgical hymn, calling us to forgiveness and reconciliation.

Soon all the children were singing and we did not look back. Instead we walked all the way back to Jish, past the wildflowers and almond trees. That evening Israeli television carried my whole speech to the soldiers. A short article appeared in the newspaper.[1]

The next day we took one hundred children and all the olive saplings to Jerusalem. Going straight to the government building, we asked a Knesset official for a place to plant our olive saplings, but were refused.

Expecting this reaction, the Committee of Biram had provided small stamped and addressed cartons. We packed each sapling in a carton and then drove to the main post office in West Jerusalem to mail the olive saplings to Prime Minister Menachem Begin, to the Knesset members, and to many other Israeli officials.

We never heard a word from anyone about the saplings, our march, or our trip to Jerusalem. It was as if we had done nothing at all.

Helping to build the school in Jish enabled me to visit my parents frequently. Mother was seventy-seven years old, Father was eighty, still living in the same room. We ate, prayed, and talked together.

Shortly before the Chrysostom Secondary School was completed, an incident occurred that apparently was due to sabotage. A sad fact in situations of power and oppression is the existence of collaborators or traitors. Unfortunately, some Palestinians are able to be bribed or co-opted by particular Jewish Israelis to give information about their fellow Palestinians or to do certain acts, such as sabotage of unwanted building projects. Sometimes, especially in the West Bank and the Gaza Strip, these collaborators are people who have been in prison and brainwashed and/or threatened into betraying their own people.

Together with eight German volunteers I was working to remove the heavy wood and metal scaffolding from around hardened concrete.

"Abuna, take care! You are in danger!" a German boy cried.

Even as he shouted, everything collapsed around me, and I was struck on the head with scaffolding. Intense pain and white flashes of light seared through my brain. I crashed to the ground, barely conscious, but visualizing the huge nails in the lumber. *O God, is there a nail in my head?*

"Poor Abuna!" I heard the German boy say as he leaned over me. "It's finished for you."

Even in my dazed condition I was annoyed that he did not go for help but merely pronounced me finished. "I'm not finished yet," I groaned, trying to move. "Bring some ice."

Others helped me out of the building, assuring me no nail was in my head. The boy brought what he thought was ice from a nearby house but in reality it was the bottom of a broken bottle. When it was applied to my head wound, I felt excruciating pain. The doctor used many stitches to close both wounds.

Upon investigation the construction crew found the scaffolding had been deliberately loosened so it would collapse when touched. Villagers told how they had spotted and then chased an unidentified man in the unfinished school the previous evening. The man escaped in a jeep. Thereafter we guarded the work site and carefully inspected the construction.

"Wisdom," I sang. "Let us be attentive." Mukhless, the lay reader, chanted the scriptural reading from the center aisle while I stood behind him in the middle doorway of the iconostasis. No musical instruments are used in the Byzantine churches. We sing and chant a cappella. When Mukhless finished, I sang, "Peace be to you, reader."

This Sunday is strange, I thought, turning to face the altar. *I am sure I smell cigarette smoke. Who on earth would smoke during the liturgy? Abu Zeidan and his family are here, even the poor, broken son. Everyone else seems restless, edgy.*

It was time to read the gospel passage. Picking up the beautiful gospel book, I chanted the preparatory prayer and walked through the left archway to go outside the altar area. The altar boys preceded me with candles and the incense burner. Once out in the center aisle, I again prayed facing the altar, holding the gospel book to my forehead in reverence.

"Save us, Son of God, we who sing you Alleluia. . . ."

Something was not right in the congregation behind me. There was muttering and shushing, the scraping of benches on the floor. Perhaps someone was ill. *I will not interrupt the liturgy,* I thought. *My parishioners will have to take care of the situation, whatever it might be.*

". . . that we may understand the announcing of your Good News. . . ."

I felt a flurry of activity to my left followed by a muffled cry and a scuffling sound, but forced myself to concentrate on the gospel prayers.

Later I learned that Zeidan had been rushed out of church by several men after he attempted to stab me with a butcher knife. Zeidan's uncle had caught his hand when the knife was only centimeters from my back.

Chapter 15

The Mount of the Ogre

At first I regarded Zeidan's attack as an accident, like the collapsed scaffolding or the kidnapping, but I, Elias Chacour, had not been the target in Jish or Beirut. When Zeidan attacked me with a knife in my own church in Ibillin, he was attempting to hurt *me*, and no one else. In a lucid moment, Zeidan tried to explain his action. "Abuna, I did not want to kill you completely. I just wanted to mutilate, wound, and slash you everywhere so you would feel how much I have suffered. I wanted you to pray to God and say that I have suffered enough."

How fragile and insignificant I really am, I thought. *How easily I could lose my life, like paper in the wind, and it could happen in such a quick, senseless way. God knows I am ready to die, but I love to live, I love this beautiful earth and God's people, and I want to be a part of it as long as possible. I want to accomplish the tasks God has given me to do. Am I not one of "God's deputies" on earth?*

My thoughts were not random reflections. I was receiving more and more verbalized threats to my well-being and my life. These threats were growing in direct proportion to the effectiveness of my work in Galilee and to the extent to which I spoke out about the Palestinian situation.

The first threat came in 1974, a strange, crazy telephone call. More calls and letters followed, warning me not to speak about certain subjects and describing the terrible things that would happen to me if I did. While the threats were unpleasant, I pitied the poor people who felt they had to make them. My own strength was building as I was compelled to live with constant uncertainty.

When I first began to travel abroad and speak out in the early 1970s, I was terribly frightened when I had to return to Israel, knowing I would face stiff Israeli inspection and interrogation, as all Palestinians do whether they are trying to leave or to enter Israel. Would I be jailed this time? I always had the dreadful impression that I was not a human being for these people.

Later, when I spoke even more loudly and met with so many people around the world, I lost my fear completely. I began to understand that it is not important to live long. What *is* important is the quality of life. What can anyone do against me? They can only kill me. So what? They will become murderers and criminals, and they will lose a friend. I have something for which I am ready to die.

I do not hate the Jewish people. I love every one of them. I pity those who have sold themselves to weapons, violence, and political ideologies that discriminate against others, but whatever the Jews might do to me or my people, it is not enough reason to hate them. Hatred is corruption. I do not choose to be corrupt with hatred. I will always protest every evil act done against me or my people, but I will never protest with the same methods they use. Though people may hate me, I will not return that hatred.

A fellow carries a stinky bucket of garbage on his head. He walks back and forth, very near you. The odor is terrible, and you are extremely bothered by this man and his stinky garbage. Finally you cannot tolerate it any longer, so you take another bucket of that same stinky garbage and put it on *your* head, doing the same as he does. This is insane! This is answering hatred with hatred, violence with violence.

If you are courageous, you say, "Okay, he is stinky. I will go and take that bucket of garbage from his head and throw it far away. I will get my hands dirty, but I will clean my neighbor and liberate myself." This is answering hatred and violence with creative love that pursues dignity, respect, and equality for everyone.

The answer to hatred and violence is a genuine, personal initiative completely independent from the reaction to violence. Respecting human rights and protecting human life should never be a reaction *to* violence but should arise out of one's love *for* human beings, *for* life.

This is the message of the Man from Galilee. Jesus Christ teaches us today, as he did two thousand years ago in this very place, that we are not to love people out of charity or for Jesus' sake, as if others were an instrument, a tool, or a tunnel to pass through to reach the goal. Rather, the other—the Jew, the Palestinian, the American, the Muslim, the Christian—is to be loved because that person is lovable as he or she is. We are to love as God loves. God's love is unconditional and sacrificial. God *is* love.

All this I have understood from my father, who taught me to love myself and the other. Loving others, breaking the cycle of hatred and violence, does not mean passivity or inaction. On the contrary, this love is creative, resourceful, energetic, dynamic. This love looks for ways to restore and preserve people's worth, dignity, and joy.

In the fall of 1978, at the time of the Jewish festival of Sukkot, the Committee of Biram brought 150 young people and adults to the first work camp in Biram. The practical goals for the week were to pour concrete in the churchyard and to begin repairing and renovating the church and school. This was simply the first step in restoring these two ruined buildings, which represented the heart of the village.

I arrived in Biram early on the first day of the work camp. Slowly I walked through the ruins, identifying my uncle's house, a cousin's store, and some of Father's olive trees. The pain was especially intense when I stood in front of my house. The roof was gone, the walls caved in, but it was still my house. I could almost hear Mother calling us to bring some firewood, or Atallah teasing me about eating too many figs. Today, however, the pain and loss did not have to be internalized or redirected in marches. Today we could actually *do* something to begin rebuilding Biram.

The committee had invited me to give the inaugural speech for this first work camp. I looked out on the group of volunteers, gathered in the dusty churchyard. Surrounding us at a distance was a small contingent of Israeli soldiers. Apparently following their orders, they were simply listening and observing. Just a few months later, they would not let us enter Biram, even to plant olive trees.

After commending the volunteers for their spirit and dedication, I became very enthusiastic and asked my listeners to join me in repeating certain promises: "I swear in the name of God and the ruins of Biram never to forget this is our village. I swear I shall rebuild these ruined stones and raise them from death to life. I swear never, ever to use the insane methods of violence to retaliate and regain our rights. I swear I will do everything to convince those who have deprived us of our homes that they cannot enjoy peace and security unless we return home. I swear that if we are not allowed to come back alive, we will come back dead, but that we *will* return to Biram. I swear we shall be united in our cause and never abandon Biram." We repeated the promises one by one, raising our hands in pledge.

As I was finishing my speech, we heard the rumble and roar of a truck entering the village. The ready-mix concrete ordered by the committee had arrived. The people were quiet, hushed, watching the truck approach the churchyard. It was a miracle in motion. This was the first truckload of concrete to enter Biram in thirty-one years.

Then a great eruption of joy and excitement broke out. Women and men were weeping, shouting, laughing, singing. It was a resurrection! "Here we are building again," they cried. "The soldiers destroyed our village but we are raising it up!" Our women began to ululate and to improvise songs about the tremendous act of God that was occurring.

Very soon the concrete was laid in the churchyard, covering the area that had been so muddy and dusty. During the rest of the week the volunteers worked on the school and the church, which were so precious to us. I do not think the synagogue Jesus attended as a child in Nazareth could have been any more beautiful than our church in Biram. Christ learned in that synagogue that God had anointed him to preach a year of liberation for the captives. That is what we wanted to preach for the people of Biram, for all the Palestinian people. Without this year, this era, of liberation for the Palestinians, I do not see how we can expect any liberation for the Jews in Israel. The one

123

liberation is vitally linked to the other. Either both the Jews and the Palestinians will be liberated or, God forbid, both will die killing each other or killing themselves and others with them.

At the end of the work camp I rejoiced with the volunteers, inspecting all the beautiful rebuilding that had been done. It was a wonderful reminder that if we want to build, we can, but we must resist evil without using evil methods. When others destroy, we build. When others curse, we bless. When others torture and we have the possibility of torturing in return, we forgive. However, as long as the oppressors have their boots on our mouths, we cannot even speak forgiveness. We must try to stand up and do something, to feel that we exist as human beings and that we have options. I choose the option of forgiveness and of creative love.

"Goodbye, Father Chacour! Thank you for everything!"

I stood outside the parish house waving at a group of Germans who were climbing into their bus. Many groups, small and large, were finding their way to Ibillin by the end of the 1970s, the result of my international speaking and teaching.

A group of forty American Jewish leaders had visited me and the Melkite church in Ibillin in 1976. They were curious to meet this Palestinian priest who willingly says, "Israel exists," but who insists that Palestinians exist, too, and need to have their own country if equal rights cannot be given in Israel. At the end of the liturgy they presented me with two silver U.S. bicentennial coins, each depicting the Liberty Bell.

"Well, my dear Jewish friends," I said in front of my whole congregation and our guests from neighboring villages, "you have given me the bells of freedom and liberty. I promise you, we will never stop ringing these bells until justice is implemented in Israel. Finally I will ring them in Biram, the destroyed village of my family. When we are able to rebuild Biram and return to it, these bells can enjoy peace and quiet."

As the busload of Germans trundled down the Ibillin hill toward the main road, I went into the parish house and found my walking stick. I needed to be alone with my Friend, to pray, to think, to reflect.

Heading down the southern side of the Ibillin hill and crossing the valley, I started walking up Jabal el Ghoul, the Mountain of the Ogre. Steep and rocky, it was generally avoided by the villagers, in part because of myths about an ogre who lived there. To me it was quiet and peaceful. I climbed nearly to the top of the hill before stopping to rest.

The view of Ibillin, the Mediterranean, Haifa, and Akko was spectacular, and I settled myself on a rock to drink in the beauty of God in Galilee. The Lord, my Friend, my Champion, was with me on this rocky hill, I knew.

Long ago I had learned that because I love God, Christ is visible to me. I can just close my eyes and see him inside myself. I can see Christ in the events unfolding around me. I see him in the faces of the people whom I encounter, with whom I speak. To me Christ is not an idea, a philosophy, a theology, or a system of thinking. Christ is not even a church. Jesus Christ is a living person, the living, loving God. He is my Compatriot from Galilee. It is only through the Church that I can find Jesus Christ, but I am afraid the church institution sometimes becomes a real obstacle to personal faith in God.

I began to wrestle with the Lord in prayer. *God! I am in great pain. It has to do with the bishop. Goodness, Lord, I do everything I can to please him, but nothing is right, nothing is enough. He seems determined to hate me, to degrade me, especially in front of others. God, how do I love this man and yet be true to what I believe is right for our church and our people? Lord, I have regarded the building of kindergartens, community centers, summer camps, and a school as a benefit to the people, as helping the bishop accomplish his mission. But to him my work competes, instead of completes. He sees it as a challenge to his authority. I do not intend that, Lord, and I have told the bishop so, but he is deaf to what I say.*

How many times have I invited the bishop to visit summer camps, or the construction sites for new buildings? When he did come to visit our summer camps, several thousand youngsters received him like royalty, but he saw it as an insult: "He receives me that well to show me that he is powerful," was the bishop's response.

I am feeling that the only thing that will satisfy my bishop is my disappearance. Would it be loving him to disappear, Lord? Or is loving him a matter of staying here and struggling with him?

With my walking stick, I began to explore the hill, poking at bushes and rocks. Some birds were flushed from their hiding places. *That's what I feel like doing sometimes—hiding, doing nothing but dispensing sacraments. I think that is what the bishop wants me to do. But loving the people means I must act out my beliefs and commitments, despite the struggles they generate. Now, Lord, I have another dream, the secondary school here in Ibillin. Should it remain only a dream? I am filled with the desire and energy to go ahead with it, to involve everyone in the village and build a place where our young people can have their chance for an education.*

Lights were coming on in the village as I walked down the Mount of the Ogre. Twilight settled around me. About two-thirds of the way down the hill I stopped to look around. It was here that the Melkite church owned about five thousand square meters of land, donated by a family many, many years ago. In fact, the legal papers and the village tradition showed that the land here on Jabal el Ghoul had been in the possession of the church for three centuries. It was steep and rocky, like the rest of the hill. Goats and sheep scrambled here to find food. Ancient olive trees grew just above the church land.

I wondered if the family that owned the land to the east of this property would consider selling it to the church. If they sold it, we would have more than ten thousand square meters here on the hill, and we could do something great with that much land.

Less than twenty minutes later I was climbing toward the top of the Ibillin hill, passing the Miriam Bawardy Community Center. The villagers believed this particular piece of land had been destined to have a building dedicated to the saint of Ibillin. Many people had tried to buy the land, but the sale never went through until I bought it for the church. A popular story in the village told how the local council had needed big stones to fill in the roads and had wanted to use the stones from this land. The council brought trucks and loaded them up with rocks and stones, but once loaded, the trucks could not move because their engines would not run. When the stones were unloaded, the engines ran perfectly. The villagers believed the stones were absolutely not to be removed from this place. My decision to dedicate the community center to Miriam Bawardy had made everything clear to the people, and no one was surprised when the center was a great success. As I spoke about the young woman from Ibillin, many people in the village began to relate to her as a human being, someone like themselves. Now we celebrate Miriam Bawardy in the community as a person who reminds us of God's presence, as a saint.

Later in the evening I stood at my window, looking at the land on Jabal el Ghoul, now completely shrouded in darkness. I had decided that the secondary school I had dreamed of for Ibillin should be built on Jabal el Ghoul. Would the village stories about the ogre make the people afraid to build anything there? *Perhaps we will have to change the name of the hill,* I thought, staring into the darkness.

Beginning tomorrow, I decided, *I will talk openly about the need for a secondary school in Ibillin. The time is now. I cannot let the bishop's lack of ideas keep us from creating a future for the young people of this village and of Galilee. Furthermore, I will never again refer to the opposite hill as Jabal el Ghoul. Together we will find a new name for the hill, a name that will gladden our hearts and tell everyone about the miracle God is about to perform in Ibillin.*

Chapter 16

Remember the Little Ones, My Son

"Your Highness, this is Father Elias Chacour."

I bowed slightly and then looked into the smiling, charming face of Queen Beatrix of the Netherlands. A private visit had been arranged by Pax Christi International when I spoke at their 1981 conference in Holland.

"Welcome to the Netherlands and to The Hague, Father Chacour," said the queen.

"I hope your Highness is not afraid of me," I said as we relaxed in a conversation corner of her office in the palace.

"No, of course not. Why should I be afraid?"

"I am Palestinian and not a terrorist. I assure you I have no bombs." Smiling, I opened my suit jacket to illustrate my words. "Rather, I am a terrorized person, but I don't know how to convince you I am terrorized."

"Why do you say that?" Interest and concern were on the queen's face.

"I am in the same situation as my Jewish brothers and sisters were forty years ago. They could not convince anyone they were not dirty. Today everyone wants to kill Palestinians. Your Highness, we are loving, caring people who want peace and opportunities for our children, just like you."

"Yes, I know that, Father Chacour, but politics can often be very dirty. Oh, your situation is absolutely impossible, unbearable. Come live with us here in Holland. We will give you everything you need."

"Your Highness, if you give me all The Hague, I will not accept it in place of one stone of my father's ruined house. That house relates me to my ancestors, to my Compatriot Jesus Christ, to all the history of my suffering people. Besides, it is not comfort that makes a person feel at home. It is only at home that a person feels comfortable."

"I understand," the queen said, "but I surely would like to do something to help you, Father Chacour. What could we do for you?"

I assured Queen Beatrix that enjoying her presence was a fine gift.

Later in the week Prime Minister Van Ijyk presented me with a beautiful bouquet of thirty-three red roses during a formal gathering. Stating that the Palestinians had suffered their own holocaust, their own Via Dolorosa, for thirty-three years, he offered the flowers as a hope the suffering would soon end. The poem "No More Tears in My Eyes," written by Fadwa Toukan, the famous Palestinian writer from Nablus, was then read in my honor.

A few months later I met Fadwa in East Jerusalem and described the reading of her poem in the Netherlands. When I asked if I could find her book in Israel, she wept.

"No, I am not allowed to have my book in Israel," she said. "It is banned."

Abu Haddad was a simple, pure-hearted Melkite Christian who rarely came to church. "Abuna, I pray at home, in the street, everywhere, but I don't want to pray in church. Don't worry, God will understand me."

This old man's front door opened directly onto a busy street in Ibillin. Every day Abu Haddad would sit on his small carpet on the ground right by his door, his feet resting in the road, happily visiting with the people passing by. When he was tired, he lay on his carpet and fell asleep.

One day when I passed, I saw my parishioner fast asleep on the edge of the street. Picking up sand, I sprinkled it all over Abu Haddad, on his face and body, and spoke in a loud, funereal voice.

"Abu Haddad, remember that you are dust and to dust you will return."

129

The old man woke up in shock. "O Lord, what is that?"

"No, it is not the Lord, Abu Haddad. It is Abuna Elias. You better come to church!"

Quickly the old man brushed his burial sand away, and I laughed as I continued on my way. How satisfying to help someone be resurrected!

My hope was to effect a resurrection of Ibillin's young people. The nine thousand residents of Ibillin reflected the demographics of the other Palestinian villages in Galilee: 50 percent fourteen years and under, 75 percent under twenty-eight. At age fourteen or fifteen, youngsters completed the eight years of formal education provided in the Ibillin public schools. Then, because we had no secondary school, the students needed to travel to Haifa, Akko, or Nazareth to continue their education. More than 75 percent did not continue. When I arrived in 1965, only about ten people in my entire Melkite community had finished secondary school. Now in 1981 the situation had not improved.

The youngsters who did not go on to secondary school became nearly illiterate. The young men usually joined the cheap labor force in Jewish Israeli society with no hope of advancement. Most of the young women married early, bearing children who also had little opportunity for education. The lack of education ensured that Palestinian young people could not be future partners with the Jews to negotiate mutual rights, dignity, security, and independence. Jewish Israeli students had ready access to secondary education, and many went on to technical schools and universities. Only a few of our village Palestinian students could even dream of such a possibility.

Elementary schools in Israel are provided by the government. However, secondary schools, grades nine through twelve, are all private, belonging to local municipalities, synagogues, rabbis, or churches. Financial support comes from private donations and from a complicated "quota system" through the Israeli Ministry of Education. Teachers' salaries can usually be paid from government money if a school qualifies for a good quota rating. The school building, furnishings, textbooks, and any extra supplies must all be financed privately. By law, students pay no tuition in a secondary school, although there can be fees for special books and tools.

The whole political and social situation of the Jews vis-à-vis the Palestinians is mirrored in Israel's secondary school system. Jewish youngsters have ready access to secondary schools that often are financed through worldwide Jewish support, a municipality, or religious organizations. In contrast, Arab Israeli young people, especially those living in the villages, have limited access to secondary schools because there is little outside support.[1]

Certainly no Jewish towns with nine thousand inhabitants would be without secondary schools for long, but no outcry is heard in Israel when Arab Israeli villages have none. In general, Arab villages do not receive the kind of help from the Israeli government that Jewish towns and villages receive, so their municipal resources to provide secondary schools are limited.[2] Furthermore, a Jewish town would be granted a building permit for a secondary school immediately; an Arab village is denied a permit.

The longer I was a priest in Galilee, the more I knew I must help the Palestinians build not only kindergartens and community centers, but also secondary schools, regardless of whether the Israeli government would grant the building permits. To wait for a permit was to continue wasting our young people's lives and to weaken our already fragile infrastructure. Continuing to accept a two-tiered, discriminatory educational system was to ensure that the Palestinian people in Israel would always be second- and third-class citizens, unable to address their own needs and secure their human rights.

For nearly two years I had been speaking about the possibility of a secondary school in Ibillin. Excitement and enthusiasm were growing. Now at the beginning of 1981 I was working with an architect to have blueprints drawn for a school on the Melkite land. These blueprints were needed to apply for a building permit. Soon a school building committee would need to be selected to coordinate the village's efforts to make the school a reality. My target date for opening the school was September 1982.

"We cannot get building permits for our houses. Why should the authorities give us a permit for a school?" Abu

Daoud asked. He had come to the parish house with several other men to discuss the secondary school project. "Without a permit the building could be demolished at any time."[3]

"That's true, Abu Daoud, but you took the risk of building a new house for your son," Abu Saleh said. "If you hadn't done that, your son, his wife, and his six children would all be living with you in *your* house!"

Everyone laughed. Abu Daoud's house was already crowded with seven other children.

"I know, I know," Abu Daoud replied. "You are right. But think of the amount of money this school will cost. Then think about having *that* demolished."

"Where will we get the money in the first place?" Abu Hassan asked.

"We will ask for donations here and for help from friends in Europe and the United States," I said. "I know people who might help."

"Might, *might!*" Abu Saleh said, slapping his knee. "I ask you, Abuna, who is going to help Palestinians in Israel? Everyone in the West thinks we are trying to drive the Jewish people into the sea, when it is we Palestinians who are being driven out. It's hopeless, Abuna."

"It is precisely *because* we are being driven out that we must build this school, Abu Saleh!" Karam argued. "We cannot and will not leave, but so far we have just watched the government take our land and villages. Now we have a chance to *do* something, to make the statement that we and our children and our children's children are here to stay, and that by God we will be educated and fight for our rights!"

"Hear, hear!" the other men cheered, clapping their hands.

"Just remember," Karam shouted over the din, "we are Israeli citizens with rights to education. We must claim those rights here in Ibillin!"

"Absolutely! Hear, hear!"

With their spirits high, the men agreed we would only ask for donations to cover the cost of building materials. The labor and expertise would come from the villagers themselves. We then named nine people to serve on the school building committee.

When the men left, it was quiet in my room, but the excitement lingered. I closed my eyes and stretched out on the bed. I could visualize a big, beautiful school with hundreds of young people from Ibillin walking up the hill to attend classes. *God, it's going to happen! I know it!*

In April 1981 I applied for a building permit for the secondary school in Ibillin, taking the school drawings, designs, and other necessary documents to the office of the Ministry of Interior Affairs in Akko.

Two weeks later the building permit was refused. "You will never have a permit," I was told. "The building is too expensive, the land you propose to use is agricultural land, and it is not destined for your use."

These reasons were very puzzling. That rocky, steep mountain was considered agricultural land? Incredible. Not destined for our use? Our papers showed ownership for three centuries. Too expensive to build? That was our problem, not theirs. You will never have a permit? *Goodness*, I thought, *what do I need more, a permit or a school?*

The next step was to level and grade the land on the steep hill.

The summer twilight was settling over Jish as three nuns and I approached my parents' one-room home.

I knocked on the partially open door, hearing their voices inside. No one answered the knock. Quietly we entered and found Father and Mother seated side by side on the floor with their backs to the door, saying their evening prayers. The Little Sisters of Jesus from Nazareth sat on Father's simple chairs as we listened to the two old people pray.

Fifteen minutes later Father began improvising, praying earnestly for the Israeli government to rule according to God's will, giving up persecution and oppression. Father prayed for the church, the bishop, and his own parish priest. He prayed for

133

his children, including Chacour, who had died twenty years earlier of sunstroke. Then he ended with a prayer for his priest son, asking God to protect him from becoming a lover of money and to enable him to reflect the presence of Jesus among the people.

Tears ran down my face. I remembered this same precious voice praying for me when I was a tiny child, barely walking around Father's knees. *God, make me worthy to be the son of this man and this woman who taught me to love you. May I be your reflection, as they are your reflection to me.*

"I heard you knocking on the door," Father told us when he finished praying, "and I knew you were sitting here. I did not speak with you because I was speaking to someone much more important."

Together we enjoyed sweets and Arabic coffee. Even at the age of eighty, Mother served us energetically. She had many questions to ask about the secondary school project in Ibillin. "Always remember the little ones, my son," she said. "Remember the children. They are the most important."

Shortly after our visit, I received an early morning telephone call from Father. Mother had died during the night. She had not been sick, Father sobbed, or all of us children would have been called. Instead she slept peacefully away into the arms of her Lord.

After the funeral in Jish, we buried Mother's body in the Biram cemetery. Two weeks later I happened to go to Biram and made the horrifying discovery that Mother's grave had been desecrated and her body was out in the open. Quickly I called for help and reburied the body. To this day I do not know what happened. Was it the work of grave robbers, interested in any fresh grave? Or was it the work of militant Zionists who didn't want even a dead Palestinian returning to Biram?

Father could not remain in Jish alone. At the age of eighty-two he moved to Haifa to live with his children, leaving the room in which he had dwelled for more than thirty-three years as a refugee.

"You are foolish even to think about building a school that has not been approved by the Israeli government, Abuna Elias," my bishop said. "You are also foolish to openly criticize the government for its policies in relation to Arab villages in Galilee. From what I hear, you make these statements not only here in Israel, but all over the world. This really must stop!"

I felt anger rising despite my efforts to remain calm. My visit was to inform the bishop of our project and ask for a contribution from the diocese. "Bishop, in the first place my statements are statements of fact about the educational system and the policies of Israel toward Palestinians. In the second place, I am a Palestinian priest in a Palestinian village with Palestinian people who are being wronged and oppressed. It is my duty to speak on their behalf, especially since they are unable to do so themselves. It would be wrong *not* to protest their maltreatment. And third, why aren't *you* speaking out on their behalf? Why aren't *you* interceding with the Israeli government for the building permit we need? I respect you as my bishop, but I cannot obey your order to stop speaking." I was trembling with rage.

The bishop was angry, too. He stood behind his desk and continued to demand that I be silent, implying that my salary might be in jeopardy.

"Bishop, I refuse to stop speaking out on behalf of my people in spite of your order. From now on, I also refuse to take any salary from you. I must be free to speak the truth. It's better that I depend on my parishioners to supply my needs than to be silenced for the sake of your money. I hereby declare myself free from any financial connection with you. Furthermore, I hereby withdraw the opportunity I offered you to be a part of this exciting, important project." My voice was strong but my knees were like rubber. These were incredibly risky steps.

The bishop shook his head and sat down once again behind the desk. The interview was over.

Nine faces registered disappointment and discouragement as I informed the committee about the latest refusals for financial help. The only funds in the treasury were ones the people of Ibillin had themselves contributed.

135

I was becoming discouraged, too. Most of the responses wanted us to prove we were not terrorists. People cannot prove they are not terrorists while they are being terrorized, living under oppression and injustice. Being accused of terrorism terrorizes them even more. People outside the situation rarely can see or comprehend what is truly happening.

"If we are going to open the school in September, we must begin building very soon," Karam said. "What should we do? Where do we turn?"

Whom could I talk to that I had not already contacted? Who would care enough to give us a chance? Who would believe we were not terrorists but simply wanted to educate our children?

"Wait a minute! I have an idea!" I shouted.

"You do? What?" nine people demanded.

I smiled broadly. "We are going to write a letter to the queen!"

Chapter 17

Get Up, Go Ahead, Do Something, Move!

 "You are joking! It's impossible!" exclaimed Mr. Shmueli, the director general of the Israeli Ministry of Education. We were standing in the village, and I had just pointed out the school site on the opposite hill.

"No, I am not joking. You can see where we have begun cutting the hill and leveling the ground. The cuts are twenty meters high in some places."

"But do you think you have the army at your service to take the building materials way up there? There is no road for trucks."

"Nevertheless," I insisted, "that is where we will build our school."

"Impossible. If in five years you can make a road up there, I will congratulate you."

"Don't give me five years for a road. Give me two years, and we will give you a school, Mr. Shmueli. On that hill."

Three men from the Inter-Church Coordination Committee (ICCO) in the Netherlands were welcomed in Ibillin with great hospitality. They represented the Christian group that had agreed to give us the money to purchase the building materials for the school. Queen Beatrix and the prime minister of Holland had recommended our project, and now this delegation had come to meet us, see the proposed building site and blueprints, and investigate the actual cost of building materials.

Shortly after the delegation returned to Holland, we received the glorious news that ICCO had approved a gift of 1,200,000 floren, approximately $400,000.

We in Ibillin knew beyond a doubt that we had experienced a miracle of God. God willing, students would begin classes in September at Prophet Elias High School. The school was named for the Prophet Elijah, my namesake, who is venerated by Jews, Muslims, and Christians alike. He spoke out strongly, without fear, against idolatry and oppression. The school would be Ibillin's strong statement and tangible provision for the human and God-given rights of our children in this society.

While most people in Ibillin were solidly in favor of building the school, there were some strong opponents, too. There were also many who questioned the wisdom of building without the Israeli government's approval. The fear of retribution was very great.

My own credibility was constantly tested. Others had made promises before that later were forgotten. This was Abuna Elias who was promising a secondary school and working with them to make it a reality, but all the same, there was a pervasive suspicion of once more being misled. I knew I absolutely must deliver what I had promised. Every moment I was in prayer to God to help me fulfill the expectations and hopes I had dared to raise.

"Abuna! The police are coming!" Hanni shouted from his vantage point on the steel frame of the school. About thirty men were building the wood scaffolding to hold the steel mesh into which the first-floor concrete would be poured. We hurried outside and watched a jeep crawl up the hill.

Actual construction had begun in January when the first trucks delivering steel rods, sand, cement, lumber, and tools drove between the olive trees and down the new dirt road to the building site. Hundreds of people in Ibillin were giving themselves tirelessly to the project. Karam was the foreman, driving

138

his taxi in the morning and then working at the school. Hanni, an elementary teacher, was giving all his free time to the project. Young people came to help, often forming bucket brigades for sand, water, and wet concrete. Zada organized them, helping us all.

Now in the second week of March the steel frame was up, the ground level nearly completed. Our school, eventually to be 630 square meters and five stories high, was becoming visible from the Ibillin hill. Some of the villagers' doubts were disappearing.

"Who is responsible here?" an officer demanded, climbing out of the jeep.

"It is I," I said in Hebrew, stepping forward.

"Where is your building permit?"

"I don't have one."

The policeman looked at the building and at me. "How can you build without a building permit?"

"Sir, I don't build with permits. I build with sand, cement, with cinder blocks, steel, and wood, not with permits."

"But you cannot *do* that. You cannot build without a permit in a democratic, civilized country."

"If this country were civilized and democratic, you would have given me a permit for a school long ago. I applied and you refused. We need a lot more schools in Israel so you can learn to give permits in the future."

"This is not my problem," the officer said. "You have to stop the work. All your men must come with us to the police station."

"No," I said emphatically. "I will come with you, because I am the only one responsible. These are all volunteers, working without pay."

"We do not want you. I have the order not to touch you, because you are liable to make international political difficulties."

Israeli police have something in common with American, Russian, Palestinian, and even Nazi police. Everywhere, unmistakably, behind the uniform is a human being. The problem is how to strip the uniform from the officer to discover the humanity and the beauty. Sometimes the humanity is nearly suffocated by the uniform, as in Nazi Germany. Nevertheless, we teach our children that even when Jewish Israeli soldiers are humiliating, torturing, and killing Palestinians, as in the West Bank and the Gaza Strip, there are human beings behind the ugly faces and uniforms of the soldiers. The problem is how to strip away the atrocities and the violence, converting these soldiers to the beautiful persons they can be.

We Palestinians as a people do not believe in violence and in terror. The world, however, has dressed us in terrorist clothing and we need to be stripped so people can see we are human beings who are terrorized.

The thirty men from Ibillin were taken to the police station in Shefar-Am. When questioned, they said they were volunteers, and it wasn't polite to ask whether or not the priest had a permit for the building. Revealing their humanity, the police released the men the same day.

Two weeks later the police came again, this time arresting more than forty workers and releasing them. The game continued for two months. In all, four groups were taken to Shefar-Am, the largest being seventy-five men, all from Ibillin. None of them was jailed, but the harassment sent fear and doubt rampaging through the village.

"Abuna, we will all be punished for this! We'll lose our land!" one villager said.

"Quit dragging us into your dream and making our life like hell," cried another.

"You promised us a school, but you won't keep your promise."

"Please, Abuna, just let us go back to having a quiet village."

The fear, anger, and opposition were directed at me as the one who had spearheaded the effort. I accepted that responsibility, but I felt very isolated. Some of my fellow priests were knowingly nodding their heads, saying "I told you so." I could tolerate the police and government opposition, but it was agonizing to have my parishioners, fellow villagers, and priest compatriots against me.

Many nights I was awake, praying, praying. *God, I know this is right, but everything is falling apart around me. What should I do? Call off the project? Wait for a better time? Push harder for a permit? Keep building without a permit? Call for international help?*

"Don't worry, Abuna," Karam would say. "You are doing something great, something for the community and for God. If necessary, I will sell my home to finish the school. This is my dream that I dream with you."

Sister Gislaine, Sister Nazarena, and Abuna Awad prayed daily for me and the school. The sheikh was quietly encouraging.

The ones called communists in the village, the "bad guys," soon rallied to my side. They did not represent doctrinal communism; rather they were part of the Palestinian element that protests social injustice. That element crosses all church and mosque lines.

Through all the turmoil we continued building. Many villagers were willing to face the authorities with me. In the midst of the police raids and the tremendous fear in the village, we poured the concrete for the first floor, a significant juncture in any building project. Benjamin, a carpenter, brought a lamb so we could celebrate. Although it was Good Friday, we slaughtered the lamb on the fresh concrete, a traditional blessing for the building.

"This is no more Good Friday," I proclaimed. "We are pouring concrete, we are building this school despite all efforts against us, and we are resurrecting. I hereby baptize this Good Friday as Easter Sunday! We will celebrate and eat!"

The roasted lamb provided a big meal for the sixty or seventy people on the site that day. Because we were pressured by the police, we did not stop working for any holy days, including Sundays. The offering of the lamb was a welcome moment of joy in the midst of mounting difficulties.

Shortly after Easter the police chief of all Galilee arrived in Ibillin in his official car and came directly to the parish house, asking for me. I received him in the living room of my new second-floor apartment.

The chief was very angry, stalking around the room. "Father Chacour, I have come to ask you when this comedy will finish."

"Which comedy is that?"

"The comedy of building a school without a permit. You are ridiculing all of us in Israel."

"Sir, this comedy will finish as soon as the building is ready."

"No. I am giving you the order to stop right now."

"I cannot stop. I am not building a weapons factory or a prison. I am building a school so our children can be educated and learn how to live in dignity and peace. The responsibility is yours, because you will not issue a permit." I tried to calm my racing heart and twitching muscles.

"That is none of my business. I am ordering you to stop."

"I am sorry, but we will continue. Put me in prison if you will."

The chief sighed in exasperation and shook his head. "Do you want me to imprison the whole village?"

"Go ahead, do it. I will bring international volunteers to help."

"That's it! *Stop building now!*" the police chief thundered.

"Okay, sir. Thank you. I have received your order. Go to your office, do whatever you see fit."

The police chief stormed out of my living room and down the two flights of stairs to his car.

My legs were weak and I collapsed in my desk chair. *What was I thinking of, volunteering to go to prison, daring him to imprison the whole village. God, now what? Now what?*

One week later I placed an anonymous telephone call to the police station. "Come and see that insubordinate priest. He does not obey your orders. Now he has international volunteers helping him build the school!" We had been able to make arrangements for a group of eighteen young people from Switzerland to come help us build the school for a few weeks.

The next day the police came to Ibillin with two vans and drove up the hill to the building site. The lead officer called to the blond young people who were working on the second level of the school. "You there! Come down here! You must go to the police station with me." The young people looked uncertainly at each other and then began climbing down.

"Are you actually arresting Swiss citizens?" I asked incredulously. "For doing nothing but volunteering to build a school? You will be in trouble with your boss when we make an international crisis about this."

The police officer appeared uncertain as the eighteen young foreigners lined up in front of him.

"Why don't you first ask them who they are, and then decide what to do with them?" I suggested.

The officer began to ask questions. Not one of the Swiss volunteers gave his or her name. Instead, as instructed, they answered with information about their families. Fathers were named as lawyers and professors, mothers as journalists and government officials.

The policeman took the other officers aside for a conference, then went to his car to call the police station on his wireless. "We have a problem here. Those volunteers? They are good people. We cannot arrest them. They are not Arabs."

A few days later I received a letter ordering me to court at the end of April. I slept well for the next two weeks, because the school would not be demolished before my court appearance. Afterward, maybe, but not before.

Knowing Aramaic, the language of Jesus, has greatly enriched my understanding of Jesus' teachings. Because the Bible as we know it is a translation of a translation, we sometimes get a wrong impression. For example, we are accustomed to hearing the Beatitudes expressed passively:

> Blessed are those who hunger and thirst for justice, for they shall be satisfied.
> Blessed are the merciful, for they shall obtain mercy.
> Blessed are the pure in heart, for they shall see God.
> Blessed are the peacemakers, for they shall be called children of God.

"Blessed" is the translation of the word *makarioi*, used in the Greek New Testament. However, when I look further back to Jesus' Aramaic, I find that the original word was *ashray*, from the verb *yashar*. *Ashray* does not have this passive quality to it at all. Instead, it means "to set yourself on the right way for the right goal; to turn around, repent; to become straight or righteous."

How could I go to a persecuted young man in a Palestinian refugee camp, for instance, and say, "Blessed are those who mourn, for they shall be comforted," or "Blessed are those who are persecuted for the sake of justice, for theirs is the kingdom of heaven"? That man would revile me, saying neither I nor my God understood his plight, and he would be right.

When I understand Jesus' words in the Aramaic, I translate like this:

> Get up, go ahead, do something, move, you who are hungry and thirsty for justice, for you shall be satisfied.
> Get up, go ahead, do something, move, you peacemakers, for you shall be called children of God.

To me this reflects Jesus' words and teachings much more accurately. I can hear him saying, "Get your hands dirty to build a human society for human beings; otherwise, others will torture and murder the poor, the voiceless, and the powerless." Christianity is not passive but active, energetic, alive, going beyond despair.

One day two bats fell into a pot of milk. The pessimistic bat said, "What can I do? Will I struggle and sink, and die so very tired? I will not die tired." He sank and drowned immediately.

The optimistic bat said, "I will strive to the end, and at least they will say I tried everything." She struggled and struggled, trying to fly, until she fainted. Later she awakened and found herself resting safely on a big roll of butter. This is not giving in to despair, but going beyond despair.

"Get up, go ahead, do something, move," Jesus said to his disciples.

Chapter 18

The Mount of Light

"Your honor, this priest has flagrantly violated the law in building without a permit. Even after repeated orders to stop, he and his workers continue to build, and it is now up to the second floor. We ask your honor to order this illegal building destroyed immediately." The police lawyer in the Akko courtroom made his case quickly and plainly.

The Israeli judge sat behind his high desk and regarded the group of people gathered in front of him on this day in late April 1982. Several men representing the police and the government were seated at a table to the right. Dressed in my priest clothes, I sat at a table on the left.

"What sort of building is this?" the judge asked, adjusting his glasses and peering at the papers before him.

"They say it is a school, your honor."

"You want to blow up a school?"

"It is an illegal building. No permit has been granted."

"Father Chacour," the judge finally said, taking off his glasses, "you are building without a permit. This is a very serious matter. What do you have to say to the court?"

I stood up and focused my attention on the judge, ignoring the police. "Your honor, our children's education is, indeed, a very serious matter, yet the authorities refuse to grant a permit to build a school. Your honor, I request time to find a good lawyer. An international crisis about this problem could create many difficulties. We do not need more stains on Israel's reputation. Therefore, I need time to find an excellent lawyer to help us all."

"How much time? Three months? Four months?"

145

I hesitated, not sure what to say.

"Five months?" the judge asked. "Father Chacour, I give you five months to find a lawyer and return to court. Then I want to close this file once and for all." The judge stood, nodded at us, and left the courtroom.

Five months! We could finish the school in that time! Young people would already be studying when I returned to court in the fall. What's more, the police could not demolish the building in the meantime because the judge had intervened. Praise to God!

"Père Chacour, building permits are required in France and sometimes are difficult to obtain," the Frenchwoman said. "Why is your situation any different? Why are you as a priest willfully breaking the law by building without a permit?"

The group of one hundred French pilgrims sat in the front half of the church this Sunday in June 1982, listening to me speak in French about our life as Palestinians in Israel. After I had told the story of our half-completed school, the woman raised her questions. She seemed genuinely interested but could not relate our experience to her own.

"Madame, as a priest I am called to serve God and my community. Following in Christ's footsteps, I try to bring healing to my people's lives, taking seriously the wounds and pain caused by physical, social, and political factors. I would not be God's servant if I disregarded these things, encouraging my people to be mutely passive in the midst of oppression.

"Arab Palestinians in the state of Israel are second- and third-class citizens. Take the matter of building permits. As you say, permits are required in many countries. That is for the well-being of all the people. However, when the issuance or nonissuance of a permit is based on the identity of the people making application, this is racism and oppression.

"In Israel, anyone wishing to build or remodel must apply for a building permit. Jewish people in Jewish towns and villages are able to get these permits. Jewish people who are settling on land taken from Arab villagers are able to get permits to build and to erect prefabricated houses. However, when

Palestinians apply for building permits in any city or in Arab villages, they are almost never granted without a lot of hassle, and frequently are denied.[1]

"Like every other people on earth, we Palestinian Israelis need houses to live in, schools for education, and public buildings to serve our community needs. For instance, a couple wants to be married. Where will they live? With the man's parents? There is a limit to how many people and generations can live in one house. Think of the health, emotional, and family problems that can result. The couple may decide to remodel or add on to the parents' house or to build a new house despite the lack of a permit. Now they live in constant fear of demolition, fines, and imprisonment. Just here in Ibillin a minimum of 150 couples are married each year. Many others do not marry because of the housing problems. Imagine those problems multiplied by the thousands in our villages in Galilee.

"A building permit may seem inconsequential, but its denial causes both immediate and delayed problems. People who build without permits are prone to quietism, dependency, and co-optation in order to protect their property from the authorities.[2] If we do not build schools, we remain ignorant with no hope for a better societal, economic, or political future.

"Can I, as a priest, counsel my people never to build a house, a school, or a community center because they would be breaking Israeli laws? Or must I recognize the evil in the intent and interpretation of these laws and protest in every nonviolent way possible? Remember, human laws are not always right.

"The majority of Palestinian farming land in Galilee has been confiscated by the government for exclusive Jewish use. Oftentimes a new Jewish settlement will spring up on the confiscated Palestinian land. This is all part of a project called 'the Judaization of Galilee' that is intended to break up the concentration of Arabs through Jewish settlements.[3] These settlements are surrounded by barbed wire, police dogs, and weapons. One of these settlements is just two kilometers from this church.

"If you ask the Israeli authorities about their reasons for the confiscation of Arab land and the denial of building permits to Arab Israeli citizens, you will hear about the many laws regarding land and buildings that justify the activities. The possession

147

of authority enables distortion of the right, and wronging of the powerless.

"From my experience, the reasons behind the legalities seem to be rooted in what I call 'the dark side of Zionism.' In the great effort to provide a safe, secure homeland for the Jews, a desire has emerged to completely 'redeem' the country by gradually pushing out the Arab Palestinians.[4] In 1948 many Palestinians fled or were chased out of their villages, most of them leaving the new state of Israel. At that time my family became refugees, but we managed to stay inside Israel, close to our village and land. Now the push is gradual and insidious, and it takes many forms, such as land confiscation and denial of building permits.

"Perhaps you can see," I concluded, "why we feel ourselves under so much pressure and why we look for positive, non-violent ways to resist the laws that we believe are designed to push us out of our villages and land. Being a priest among Palestinian people living in Israel does not mean blindly keeping oppressive human laws but rather asking God for the wisdom to pursue actively what is just and right for all human beings. As I have said to the police and other Israeli authorities, 'Let me build a school now and save you from having to build a prison later.' "

The school construction was now proceeding nearly non-stop. Volunteers came at five o'clock in the morning; by midnight, workers were still watering the fresh concrete and preparing cinder blocks, wood, and tiles for the early morning workers. We trucked in the water and dragged an electrical cable seventy-five meters up the hill from the nearest home.

At night I could locate the school from my apartment window by the tiny, beautiful light on the hill. It spoke to me of Christ, the Light of the world, and his words about a light on a hill not being hid. I vowed to keep a light burning on top of the school when it was finished as a proclamation of our victory over illiteracy and divisions in Ibillin.

The days of construction were joyous but increasingly difficult for me physically. I slept little and worked on the construction whenever I could be away from parish duties.

Hauling, lifting, pushing, shoveling, climbing, bending—whatever was needed I did. As the summer wore on, I could feel my body wearing out. At the age of forty-two my back, kidneys, and hips were protesting mightily at the constant wear and tear.

As the school administrator, I also needed to hire teachers and clerical staff, order books, purchase furnishings, and raise money from our friends overseas to pay for all these things. I pushed very hard because my one goal was to open the school on September 1. Ignoring the warning signals my body was giving, I strained toward that goal. By the end of August I was physically broken. Every step was painful, and I could barely stand upright due to my aching hips and spine.

Nevertheless, I stood at my window each night and gazed at the pinpoint of light. The opposite hill was no longer Jabal el Ghoul. It was Jabal Ennuur, Mount of Light.

On September 1, 1982, I stood on the wide entry porch of the school's main door and rang a little bell. Behind me were five teachers, and in front of me was the most beautiful sight I had ever seen: ninety-two boys and girls from Ibillin, Muslims and Christians, were gathered. Their smiling faces were bright and filled with anticipation. I welcomed them, introduced the teachers, gave instructions about our daily schedule, and assigned them to their homerooms. Then we thanked God together for our beautiful Prophet Elias High School on the Mount of Light. In a few moments the students entered the building, carrying pencils, notebooks, and a lunch in their backpacks, eager to learn. Their happy voices filled the halls, making a real school of the steel and concrete.

O God, I thought as I followed the young people into the school, *if I die now, I will not regret it. It was worthwhile to be born for this moment.*

Slowly Mr. Shmueli emerged from his car, his eyes glued to the five-story school building, a look of utter amazement on his face. Earlier in the day I had telephoned the director general of the Ministry of Education, inviting him to visit. Together we toured the inside and outside of the building, greeting the students and staff. Finally we rested, leaning on his car and gazing at Prophet Elias High School.

"Father Chacour, this is a miracle. If you tell me that tomorrow the resurrection will take place, I will believe you!"

"No, no, Mr. Shmueli, I do not need to tell you about the resurrection," I said, laughing. "What I do need is a good quota rating from you so we will have enough money to pay our teachers."

"What do you want, Father Chacour?"

"I want a 100 percent quota." The Israeli Ministry of Education must pay funds per capita to every secondary school according to the number of students and the quality of services given to those students. I wanted the maximum amount possible.

The director general was aghast. "Impossible! No Jewish school in Israel gets 100 percent! How can you even ask for that?"

The bargaining that ensued finally resulted in a 91.4 percent quota, far higher than most schools in Israel.

"There is one more thing I want, Mr. Shmueli—a building permit."

"That is out of my hands, I'm afraid. I will deal with you as I would any other school, but that is the best I can do."

"Thank you for that, and thank you for coming to see the school."

"I had to see this for myself. I'm still not sure I believe my own eyes!" The director general slowly drove down the steep road, peering at the school rising above him to his left.

"Where is your lawyer, Father Chacour?" The judge frowned as he opened the court session in Akko at the end of September 1982.

"I found many lawyers, your honor, but they are so expensive that I decided to defend this cause by myself."

"Very well. The court will hear the argument of the prosecution."

The lawyer for the police and the government stated that no building permit had been granted and that the school, now fully built and in use, was illegal. He requested the destruction of the building as an example to others who would try to defy the government. He also requested that I be punished for my role in building the school.

"Father Chacour, what is your defense to these charges?" the judge asked.

God, give me the words that will convince this man we are simply human beings who need this school for our children, I prayed.

"Your honor, you have the power to destroy this building, but you will have to destroy it on the heads of the one hundred Israeli citizens who are learning in that school. If that happens, I will be forced to go all over the world telling what you have done and begging for money to build a new school. I know I could raise millions of dollars, but then I will further stain Israel's reputation, and we don't need that, do we? Wouldn't it be better to destroy a prison and let me continue working in this school?"

"This is such an ugly situation," the judge said, glowering at all of us in the courtroom. "What do you offer as a solution, Father Chacour?"

"Sir, it is so simple. You can order the government to sign a small paper legalizing this illegal building, and I will go all over the world preaching the goodness of Israel and its laws and justice. Then we will all stay friends. It is so simple!"

"No! Absolutely not! The building is illegal and must be destroyed," a government representative protested.

The judge sighed deeply. "Father Chacour, please step outside the courtroom. I need to discuss a few things with these gentlemen."

Out in the hallway I paced and prayed, prayed and paced. *O God, make hearts of stone into hearts of flesh. May your compassion speak to the human being in the judge.*

I was called back into the courtroom in only five minutes.

"Ah, Father Chacour, thank you for waiting," the judge said. "This is indeed a delicate and intricate circumstance, but we have come to an agreement."

My heart was pounding and I was barely breathing. *What will I tell my people if the judge rules that the school must be demolished?*

"Father Chacour, you will never have a permit for the building, but the school will not be destroyed. I know you were hoping for the permit, but that is impossible. However, I wish you well in running your school in the building you have."

"Thank you, your honor!" I considered this a great victory. So what if we did not have a permit? The school was safe from demolition!

"I am curious, Father Chacour." The judge had now relaxed, becoming very informal. "You have your building, but without a permit you have no utility services. How will you manage without water, for instance?" The police and government representatives were listening to the conversation.

"Sir, I already have water by the village authority, and you cannot turn it off. Only the Supreme Court of Justice in Jerusalem can do that."

"All right, but how will you manage without electricity?"

"Your honor, we can use petrol lamps if necessary, but we hold school during the daytime, not at night. We can see perfectly well." In fact, we were still using the one electrical cable we had dragged from the nearest house during the construction.

"But surely you need a telephone?" the judge persisted.

"Your honor, I have a telephone in my home. I am lucky if it works three days in a month. I might have a heart attack with another phone like that! But I have the Arabic telephone, mouth to mouth, and that's *never* out of order!"

The judge laughed uproariously and then came to shake my hand, wishing me well. He was very human, with a heart made of flesh.

The judge was right, of course. Operating the school without a permit was going to challenge all our patience and ingenuity.

That electrical cable, for instance. How many times a day did students drag that cable to the second floor, then to the fourth, then back to the first? When they complained, I said to them, "You do not have electricity because you do not have a permit. You do not have a permit because you are Palestinians. Just remember—whenever you have the upper hand over any person or any group, Jew or Palestinian, do not use the same methods that are used against you. It is so ugly, so corrupting, to

152

the one who is oppressive. Use human and humane methods to tame the other, rather than stirring up anger and bitterness." Then, as a team, we together dragged that heavy, aggravating, cumbersome, precious electrical cable.

Chapter 19

For Sale: One Permit

Israel invaded Lebanon in June 1982 while we were building our school. In September we heard the dreadful news of the massacres in Sabra and Shatila refugee camps. All too vividly I remembered the hours I had spent at Sabra camp in 1975. Now we were mourning the deaths of perhaps three thousand men, women, and children, slaughtered by the Lebanese Phalangist army as the Israeli army surrounded the camps.[1]

Word also came that Amira, my nineteen-year-old cousin, was killed in a bombing in Beirut. One of the Israeli jets that streaked north over Ibillin every day in the summer of 1982 carried the U.S. manufactured vacuum bomb that murdered Amira. The building she was in was sunk three meters underground. More than two hundred Palestinians were buried forever in the ruins.

Remembering the beautiful girl and her happiness when I had visited Dbayeh refugee camp, I wept and wept, horrified, angered, saddened. Finally I rose from my tears more determined than ever to help create a bright future for Palestinian young people in Galilee.

The holocaust in Europe was so horrible, lasting four long years, but the Palestinian holocaust has already lasted forty years. Those who survive suffer much more than those who are killed. It must end before there is a total moral corruption of the Jews in Israel, and before a similar corruption occurs among the Palestinians. God help us all.

154

"I must take a gift," my father said. "It is unthinkable to visit the pope with empty hands. But what can I take him?"

Love for Father welled up inside me. This poor Palestinian peasant wanted to take a gift to the man who administers the Catholic church's great wealth and is, for many people, God's deputy on earth.

"What do you want to take, Father?"

"Ah, I don't know."

"Don't take anything. It's not necessary."

"You do not tell me what to do. I will do what I want."

All of us in Atallah's living room laughed. Even at eighty-three, Father was certain to do what he wanted. After some initial hesitation, he had decided to go to Rome for the beatification of our saint from Ibillin, Sister Miriam of Jesus Crucified. Unbeknownst to us, the Vatican had been investigating her life for many years. Now, in March 1983, the magnificent beatification ceremony would take place and be attended by Melkite bishops from all over the world. As the priest from her hometown of Ibillin, I had been invited to attend, but I was scheduled to speak to the Swedish Parliament the very same day. I made arrangements for Father to go with the rest of the delegation from Galilee. Now he was looking forward to his first plane ride and a meeting with the pope.

Shortly before Father left for Rome, he called me to come to Haifa. When I entered Atallah's living room, Father was smiling broadly, jittery in his excitement to show me the box he was holding.

"Come see, my son! Come see the gift I am taking to the pope!" Father made me sit beside him on his daybed and then handed me the precious gift. It was a beautiful olive wood box covered with mother-of-pearl.

"It is truly excellent, Father!" I admired the box from all sides.

"Open it! See what I put inside!"

Carefully I opened the box. There lay a photograph of the ruins of our church in Biram.

"I want the Holy Father to see Notre Dame, my son, and know the story of our village." Father's eyes were shining.

After the beatification one of my cousins told me how Father had been chosen by the Galilee entourage to present his gift to the pope.

"You would have been so proud of him, Abuna! Your father handed the pope the olive wood box and told him about the photograph. 'Your Holiness, St. Peter is still standing but our Notre Dame is destroyed. Can you do anything so we can rebuild it in Biram?' The Holy Father visited with him a moment before shaking hands with all of us from Galilee. All the while, many photographs were being taken."

Father gave me a copy of his prize photo showing himself with the pope. Here was the proof that Mikhail Chacour, an old peasant from Galilee who still would ride his donkey if he were living in Jish, had flown to Rome and met the pope. This was, for Father, like seeing someone only a little less holy than God. He had told that person about his greatest heartache, the loss of his village and his church.

I framed the photograph and hung it on the wall in my office. Whenever anyone asked me about it, I said it was a picture of the holy father with the pope.

Father had done his part in telling the pope about Biram. I, in the meantime, was busy telling the Swedish Parliament about the absolute, vital need for negotiations between Jews and Palestinians. I told about our struggle in Galilee and about the suffering of our brothers and sisters living under Israeli military occupation in the West Bank and Gaza, and still others scattered in Lebanon, Syria, and Jordan. Then I explained that if we could not live together equally as Jews and Palestinians in one state, we needed to have two states side by side, Israel and Palestine.

When I returned to Israel, I received a late night telephone call. "Everything you said in Stockholm was known to us before you arrived at Ben Gurion Airport."

I immediately recognized the rough, angry voice of a policeman I knew.

"If you continue to speak, your life will be very short, priest. Your secret police record is already extremely full with the things you have said, with everything you are doing against Israel."

My greatest sorrow, however, resulted not from the government threats but from Arab collaborators sent by my own bishop.

One night in 1983 a man from Ibillin, well known for his collaborative activity with the Jewish authorities, appeared at the parish house about nine o'clock, half drunk and extremely aggressive. This same man had often called to curse me on the telephone.

"You do not obey the bishop," he shouted. "You might be backed by international figures, Abuna, but the bishop is backed by all the local authorities. So far we haven't used that against you. The bishop wants you to stop speaking out for the Palestinians, and you had better obey him." Finally he left, leaving me feeling angry, sad, and frightened.

Since the 1982 Israeli invasion of Lebanon, we Palestinian Melkite priests had no longer felt that the bishop's residence in Haifa was our refuge or home. Instead it seemed to us to be a stronghold for the Phalangist army in Lebanon, the army that had slaughtered the Palestinians in Sabra and Shatila. I had been particularly outspoken about our outrage.

The bishop was using many avenues to silence me. He had ordered my transfer to a small, remote parish in the north of Galilee, but I refused to leave Ibillin. Shortly after, I received written orders to come to the police station in Shefar-Am for special investigation.

"I am speaking with you in the presence of a foreign ambassador in Israel," I said in a telephone call. "Why are you ordering me to come to you? Is it something to do with security or sabotage or any crime?"

"You just need to obey the order," the police official said.

"If I choose to come to the police station, I will come with lawyers and several ambassadors. Is that what you want?"

"No, no," he said after a hurried consultation with another official. "Actually, we don't want you, Abuna. Don't come, don't come. You just visit your bishop and ask him for the reasons."

When I was eleven I traveled with Father from Jish to Haifa on my first bus ride, beginning the long journey to become a priest. Father would leave me at the Bishop's School. I sat by Father feeling choked, unable to cry or speak. Going farther and farther from my family and the hills I loved, the bus traveled around many curves and corners. *How will I ever find my way back to Jish again?* I cried inwardly. *Can anybody find the way?* I didn't think so. I looked up at Father. He was so happy and proud. In his eyes I was already "little abuna."

God was calling me to be a priest, I knew, and I loved the Church. It was the one place I felt truly safe. In a sense I was, in Jesus' words, going to my Father's house, where I belonged. But I was a child, a refugee child. I had experienced homelessness ever since I left our house in Biram four years earlier, carrying only a blanket. Although I lived with my family in Jish, I longed for a home. Perhaps the Church could be that home for me. It was all frightening, exciting, risky, and confusing.

Today I still love my Melkite church in Galilee. It is dearer to me than any beloved to her lover. My life as a priest with my parish and with Christians in Ibillin and the other Galilee villages is beautiful. However, my life as a clergyman in our institutional church has been a tragic story of disappointment and of successive shocks and scandals.

As a boy, I believed priests are to be so courageous, compassionate, good, sweet, and truthful with others that Christ is made present. Now I know that is idealistic, but I cannot accept the selfishness, corruption, and hatred I have witnessed as a priest in our institutional church. *God, will our church survive this agony? What do you want me to do? I feel powerless, yet I want so much to help my people and our church.*

In the darkest moments I remember the Bible story Mother told about the prodigal son and his brother. As a child, I clearly pictured those two boys, the one running off with part of his father's fortune and the other moaning and complaining at home. I cried when Mother told that story, not for the two sons but for the poor father. He was so good, too good to be their father.

When the prodigal son returned, the father ran to meet him, something a man in our culture even today does only in a great emergency or a matter of much importance. The boy did not deserve his father's attention, but the father was not interested in doing justice to the son. He was going beyond justice, expressing his compassionate love for this lost son. He wanted to restore the son's dignity and likeness to the father. When he saw his son coming, so dirty inside and outside, the father forgot all the horrible sins and cared not for what the boy had done, but for the boy himself.

This is a picture of God's love toward every human being, incredible as it seems. Our lives are not measured by the acts we have done but rather by the depth of God's love for us and our love for God. Nothing is beyond God's love and mercy. Nothing. Not even my poor church.

The telephone rang. When I answered, a man spoke in Hebrew. "You do not have a permit for your school, do you?"

I was startled. It was October 1983 and no one had mentioned the permit for a long time. "That's correct, we do not have a permit."

"Do you want a permit?"

"Yes, of course I want a permit."

"Do you know the law of give and take?"

"Surely. I learned that when I studied the Talmud." *I also learned something else*, I thought. *Respect and suspect.* "What do you want?"

"I can bring you a permit if you will give me one thousand American dollars for my pocket."

My mind was spinning. A permit? An actual, genuine building permit from the Israeli government? Respect and suspect. "First I see the permit. If it is genuine, you have the money."

"Agreed," the unknown man said, excitement in his voice. "I will see you in a few days. Have the money ready."

I hung up the phone, stunned. Was it possible? *God, your ways are mysterious, but can this be the way we will get our permit? And where can I find one thousand dollars fast?*

159

Formulating a plan, I drove rapidly up to Prophet Elias High School. The only possible way to collect that amount of money was to involve all the students, making of the collection another teaching experience.

Although I was confident the students would bring in the money, I was uncertain of my caller's ability to bring a valid permit. The next two days I spoke to God almost constantly. I scrutinized every car and driver that passed the parish house or drove up the Mount of Light.

Late in the afternoon of the third day the man arrived at the school. He was a total stranger to me. Remaining in his car, he gave me a large envelope. I drew out a valid permit with the name of Prophet Elias High School, the official stamps, and the proper signatures all in place. It was perfectly legal and absolutely beautiful. I then handed the man a large packet, which he opened, quickly counting the money. Immediately he drove away. I never saw him again.

I was grateful to God for the permit, but I was sad, too. I did not regret the one thousand dollars. Goodness, it was just money. No, it was the horrible sense of having been abused while in a helpless, hopeless situation. We had been forced into a position of paying the unholy money because the government had blocked all the legal avenues. How much better it would have been for our students to learn about a just, democratic legal system rather than having to collect money to pay blackmail.

We have the permit, and that is the important thing now, I thought, *but wherever I go in this world to tell the story of our school, I will also tell the story of the thousand-dollar permit.*

One afternoon in the fall of 1983 the nuns called to say that a military patrol was just outside the parish house. Then I heard heavy, running footsteps on the outside stairs leading to my apartment, followed by sharp knocks on the door.

"Yes, can I help you?" I asked the armed Israeli soldier.

"Abuna Chacour, I must talk to you quickly in case the other soldiers come up." The young man with black, curly hair and alert brown eyes entered and closed the door. "You don't remember me, do you?"

"No, should I?" How would I have known this young Jewish man? Why did he call me Abuna?

"No, no, of course not," he said, shaking his head. "I just thought maybe . . . well, when I was small you played with me. You and my father were classmates at Hebrew University."

Of course! This strapping soldier was the tiny child I had so enjoyed in Jerusalem. Now he was in the army, carrying an Uzi submachine gun. "Oh, my dear boy, your name is Gideon, is it not?"

"Yes, it is Gideon, Abuna." We embraced each other, and I thought I would weep. Here was this sweet child all grown up, and he remembered me.

"Abuna, my superior officer and other soldiers are downstairs and wish to speak with you. I volunteered to bring you down. We are on a routine patrol and soon will go into Lebanon. I was very excited when I realized we were coming to Ibillin. I remembered hearing your stories about the village. Suddenly I wanted desperately to see you, Abuna, and tell you of my feelings. I know from my father and from knowing you that Palestinians are good people, not the animals so many of my friends think they are. I am required to be in the army, Abuna, but it is so important to me that you know I do not hate you or any Palestinian person. Do you believe me?" The beseeching brown eyes were filled with tears. "Please believe me!"

"Yes, of course, Gideon. Of course I believe you. May God go with you and keep you safe."

The young man again threw his arms around me, and his gun slapped me on the hip. Then he quickly released me, wiped his eyes, and opened the door. "Please, Abuna, you must come with me downstairs. It would be better if we did not know each other."

"Yes, of course." I walked ahead of him down the two flights of stairs. Waiting for us were several other soldiers. "Hello, sirs. What can I do for you today?" After visiting briefly, I learned that it was indeed a routine patrol as Gideon had said.

Chapter 20

Betrayed

"What do you think, Abuna? Does it look like a fish?"

Khalid was kneeling close to the wall, cementing small pieces of gray, tan, and black marble inside the lines that other students had drawn. I backed up a few meters and scrutinized the mosaic from a distance.

"When you finish the tail, Khalid, it will definitely be a fish!"

I was escorting a small group of guests from England around the school property. We watched Khalid and other students as they worked on the loaves and fishes mosaic. It was the newest series that had been designed and created on the cement retaining walls surrounding the parking lot behind the high school. Now in the summer of 1985 the Peace Center had been built, curving gracefully against the hill. The ground level was an open carport with benches built against the decorated retaining wall. Above the carport soared two stories of rooms, already invaluable to our school. Zada lived in a small suite on the top floor, the same level as the guest hostel that she supervised in addition to her work as school maintenance supervisor. Guests had begun coming to the hostel, meetings and discussions were held, the library was in the process of being transferred from the community center, and a great variety of activities were taking place on the Mount of Light.

"The dominant theme in the mosaics is light," I told the English people. "Here are the words 'You are the light of the world,' and here are children walking on the pathway to the sun. Over there is a man carrying a torch of light, a symbol for our school. There is a mosaic of the school itself. And here is a depiction of the powerful Prophet Elijah. See how he sits, so weak and humble, looking up at the raven, the gift of God, bringing him food. If a prophet does not depend on God but relies on his own might, he is no more a prophet.

"We are all weak and poor. Only God can give us the power to overcome hatred and bitterness. Only God can give us the compassion to face our enemy, doing everything possible to convert the enemy to a friend, and a friend to a brother or sister. Without God's love and compassion we will take the sword and kill the enemy.

"God does not kill, my friends. God does not kill the Ba'al priests on Mount Carmel or the inhabitants of the ancient city of Jericho. God does not kill in Nazi concentration camps or in Palestinian refugee camps or on any field of battle. Wherever there is killing or oppression, it is we who do it in the name of God. God is the first persecuted, the first victim of our bad deeds. God does not kill. Rather, God gives life, God forgives and goes beyond justice to compassionate love. This is what I learned from my Compatriot, Jesus Christ. He was ready to be crucified and killed to redeem poor sinners."

After leaving the visitors in Zada's care, I walked down the outside stairs of the Peace Center and into a room on the second level. There was my delight and my joy, the grotto we had carved in the Mount of Light.

As the Peace Center was being constructed, I asked the contractor to cut a doorway on the inside wall of this room. When the building was finished, some students and I began to dig into the exposed rock with hammers, picks, and our bare hands. After several months we had carved out a beautiful grotto as large as a room. Along the rounded sides we carved benches on which to sit while praying and reflecting. The door from the room in the Peace Center now led directly into the grotto deep in the Mount of Light.

The grotto was furnished with a small altar, candles, icons, and flowers. The outside door was never locked. Soon teachers and students discovered it was a wonderful place to be quiet and to pray.

After lighting the candles, I sat on a rock bench in the grotto, sighed deeply, and closed my eyes, letting myself relax.

Here in the hill it was perfectly quiet. I was alone with my Friend, my Compatriot.

As a protest, I had decided not to attend the 1985 annual priests' retreat in Nazareth. Instead, after long hours of prayer, I had decided to ring the bells of danger about the explosive and dangerous situation in our diocese. Churches and congregations were surviving only because they refused to die. We had no development projects, no pastoral plan, nothing. In private, parishioners and priests were asking critical questions about the bishop's political affiliations and his pastoral and financial administration of the Melkite church in Galilee. In his presence, however, people flattered the bishop. Once again I was about to become a Jeremiah, publicly challenging my current bishop as I had challenged Bishop Hakim twenty years earlier.

In a letter addressed to the bishop and the eighteen priests currently in the diocese, I first commended the constructive local efforts that were being made in Galilee. Then I went on to suggest a reassessment of our goals. "What is the mission that we carry to this crucified nation, the Palestinians?" I wrote. "Are we commissioned only to baptize, celebrate weddings and funerals, because people cannot have these rituals without passing under our hand? . . . The truth is that power and might are the determinant factors among us, instead of truth and justice. We are competing among ourselves, not completing each other. We try to destroy the ones who are doing something for the people. Don't we hate the one who does not say yes in everything? And the spiritual and material treasures of this diocese—aren't they directed outside the diocese rather than to its own children?"

I then went on to describe the continual misunderstandings I had had with the bishop and the deteriorating conditions I had observed in the diocese. Finally, I challenged the clergy to address the problems, and then asked, "Are you going to exile me as you exiled other priests?"

The letter was dated June 30, 1985. After making copies of the letter, I placed them in separate envelopes addressed to the bishop and the individual priests at their retreat in Nazareth. I prayed that my words would be a healing balm and not a killing bomb.

"*Axios, axios, axios.* He is worthy, he is worthy, he is worthy." The chanted words from my ordination service haunted me as I waited for the answer to my letter. Am I worthy of being a priest? The old questions were back to torture me. I was just Elias Chacour, a broken, sinful man like all others, an ordinary peasant from Galilee. Now, because I had challenged the bishop and priests with such strong words, I was thrown headlong into painful doubt. I never doubted God, God the Compassionate Father. Rather I doubted my own judgment and the wisdom and actions of the bishop and the other priests.

At the same time I was rejoicing as I experienced the reality of Christ in the midst of pain. Jesus Christ is not an idea but is a person. He is so alive, so present.

The pain and the joy, the presence of Christ and the isolation from my fellow priests, were all mixed together as the days in early July passed by. I could visualize the bishop and priests together in Nazareth. Now they were praying, now they were eating, now they were discussing this and that. Did they have my letter? What were they saying? Would I even get an answer? Would I hang in limbo forever?

The pain permeated my dreams. Suddenly I was back in 1984, reliving a frightening physical attack. Ziad, a man from Ibillin, had broken into my apartment at midnight. He was angry and drunk, and his hands were bloody. Clenching a large, jagged piece of glass, he began slashing at me.

I dodged the glass and telephoned Ziad's family. The man continued to curse me, describing the horrors that would happen to me if I did not obey the bishop. Finally, his energy exhausted, he collapsed on a sofa. I brought a damp towel to clean his bloody hands, but he only threw it away.

Soon Ziad's family came and persuaded him to go home. My front door was wrecked, and blood was spattered all over. *Thank God it is not my blood,* I thought fervently, *but poor Ziad's hands must be very painful.*

I was sure the attack was precipitated by the protests we priests had made about the bishop's behavior in the matter of the two funerals.

A great tragedy had occurred in 1984 in Deir Hanna, a village not far from Ibillin. A family of six Melkite Catholic people was killed in an automobile accident. Church custom, village tradition, and ordinary human sensitivity dictated that the bishop of the diocese should be present at the huge funeral in Deir Hanna. Our bishop, however, disregarded the needs of his own parishioners and instead went to the funeral of Major Sa'ad Haddad, the puppet commander of the Israeli-backed Lebanese Christian Phalangist army in south Lebanon, who had died on the same day.[1] Our bishop joined Israeli government officials such as Yitzhak Shamir, Ariel Sharon, and Moshe Arens, as well as many others, at Major Haddad's funeral in Lebanon.[2]

The bishop's action was a scathing slap in the face not only to the poor grieving family in Deir Hanna and to every Melkite in Galilee but also to every Palestinian. Major Haddad was regarded by all Palestinians as an archenemy. Yet our bishop abandoned his own people sorrowing in Galilee to go to Major Haddad's funeral.

In this case the priests were united in their protests, openly manifesting anger and unhappiness with the bishop. Subsequently, several priests were threatened. Ziad and his shard of glass were the answer to my outrage.

On July 6 I received a thin envelope in the mail from the bishop's office. I did not want to open it. Instead, I took it into the church and laid it on the altar. Putting on my priestly garments, I celebrated the Divine Liturgy by myself, praying every prayer, doing every ritual.

When the liturgy was over, I stood at the altar in front of God. *Lord, be the judge of my thoughts as I read this letter. If I am mistaken in this matter, convert my ideas and attitudes. If the others are mistaken, may we all convert and change. God, I know it is not a question of personal prestige but rather a question of adjustment to the message of Christ.*

Finally I opened the letter and read the few lines. Every proposal I had made was rejected; everything I had said was declared wrong.

I stared at the signatures. Every one of my priest colleagues had affixed his name to this brief letter of rejection. Not one had abstained. Not one spoke in my behalf. Not one. Even Abuna

Faraj, my friend since childhood, now almost completely crippled, had shakily signed his name. Abuna Ibrahim, the young married priest I enjoyed so much—even his name was here. So were two names of priests who don't even read Arabic, one American and one Dutch, who ordinarily stayed out of these discussions.

It was worse than I had expected. Painful abandonment gripped me. Loud cries welled up from the depths of my heart. Taking the letter, I hurried to the grotto, where I finally let my feelings come out. Weeping loudly, I begged God to forgive them and to help me forgive them, too. I pleaded with the Lord to save our church, praying for the children, the families, the old people.

Hours later, I asked God for peace and strength to carry on alone. Now I had no one to turn to except my Friend and Champion. "That is more than enough," I said aloud, blowing out the candles.

I threw myself into my parish duties in Ibillin and into the work of the enormous summer camp, but at night I often wept like one of the children I had held during the day. I did the only things I knew to do—work and pray. When I saw Father and my brothers and sister, I spoke as if everything were fine.

Not only was I busy with the summer camp, but also with weddings. July and August are the wedding season in Palestinian villages, a time when the planting is over and the harvest is not yet ready.

The wedding processions through the village streets are always delightful. All couples, Muslim or Christian, are escorted to the ceremony from their respective homes by a large singing, dancing group of villagers. After the ceremony they are escorted back to the groom's parents' home. All in all the celebration takes the better part of a day. Sometimes four or five weddings occur in a week.

At night I would remember the beautiful bride and the happy groom, thanking God for their new life together and the children who would soon be born. Then the dark thoughts would creep into my head.

Through my ordination I was married to the Church. I loved the Church and wanted to belong to it and have it belong to me. But now, in my ongoing isolation and abandonment, I was feeling like a man who had married the most beautiful woman, had conceived gorgeous children with her, had worked to give this family the very best life he could, willing even to give his life for them all, and then after twenty years of marriage had made the abominable discovery that his wife was a prostitute. Once again I wept, feeling utterly betrayed.

Ilonka offered me more coffee and *kanaafi*, a sweet dessert made of sugar and cheese. She turned to Faraj sitting in his wheelchair and held the teacup to his lips so he could sip the hot liquid. Then she took a small portion of the dessert on a fork and offered it to him. He ate it and beamed.

What a blessing this Australian woman is for Faraj, I thought for the hundredth time. Without her to assist him in every way, he would not be able to continue his work. As it was, Faraj and Ilonka, along with a small staff, operated a school, activity center, and hostel in Nazareth. In the early 1980s, Faraj had told me about his dream, and together we had found funding to construct the three-story building on a hill. Now many programs were running in the building, keeping Faraj active as a priest.

Cleaning up the dishes, Ilonka promised to be nearby if Faraj needed her, and then left us alone.

"How are you, Elias? I want the truth. This is Faraj talking."

"I am busy. There is much to do in the school and Peace Center, of course. I have been traveling quite a bit, speaking in Europe."

"That's not what I asked," Faraj persisted, his breath coming in short spurts. "You are always busy. But how *are* you?"

I sighed heavily, knowing I could hide nothing from this man. "Not very good, I'm afraid."

"Tell me about it." Faraj's kind eyes warmed me inside.

The tears insisted on springing up in my own eyes. "Oh, Faraj, that letter from all of you at the priests' retreat is so painful for me. I knew the bishop would react like that, but not all the priests. And especially not you, my friend. It hurts so badly."

"Is that why you haven't answered my telephone calls or my letters?"

I nodded, not trusting myself to speak anymore.

"Elias, let me tell you what happened at the retreat. Your letters arrived in the middle of the week, but the bishop and his aides kept them from us until the morning we were leaving. At breakfast one of the bishop's friends stood up to tell us about your letter and to distribute our copies. Then he read your letter aloud to us as we were eating. As soon as he had finished, he said, 'We reject the statements in that letter, and we have a paper already written in reply to Abuna Elias. We want you all to sign it immediately while you are sitting at the tables.' So they brought the letter around and watched each one of us while we signed."

Faraj stopped talking to catch his breath. When he continued, there were tears in his eyes, too. "Please forgive me for signing it, Elias. Truthfully, I was not clear on what I was signing, because it all happened so fast. But I should have been more careful. I should have read your letter myself and studied it, and then read the bishop's letter. Please, my friend, please forgive me."

"It is you who must forgive me, Faraj. I should never have doubted you, and I should have come when you called."

"Elias, many visitors come here, and many of the priests are rereading your letter and beginning to make their own statements and complaints to the bishop. Many of them are very afraid you will leave the diocese, and they are saying that to the bishop, too."

"Very often I have been tempted to go far away and find new work, Faraj," I replied, "but every time I decide to go, I say to myself, 'No! You will not desert. The Lord wants you here to struggle, to reform, and to give hope to your people.' If what you say is true, perhaps we as priests can struggle to make that reformation and give hope to our parishioners."

Faraj looked very tired, but his face was shining. "We'll do it, Elias, and we will do it together. You will see!"

Chapter 21

Living Stones

In early October 1985 the bishop telephoned, saying he had received letters from the priests and now wanted clarification of my June 30 letter. The priests were starting to recognize the validity of my statements and were asking themselves why they had signed the rejection letter.

I quickly set to work. The new letter, dated October 10, 1985, called for reform in the Melkite diocese—specifically, changes that would give the parishioners more involvement in the administrative and spiritual life of the church; establish a consultation community around the bishop to help with the sensitive and dangerous issues facing Melkite Christians in Israel; and help the priests with problems of tenure, communication, and relationships. Challenging the bishop to take an attitude of courage, I pledged the priests' cooperation in bringing about reforms.

Copies of the October letter were sent to all the priests. This time nearly two-thirds of them responded positively. The letter was sent to the patriarch and also read in the bishop's council.

The priests asked to meet with me regularly so we could share our concerns and the possibilities for reform. These gatherings were usually held at the Peace Center in Ibillin. The priests tried to make reforms at the parish level, but no reforms were made by the bishop. It was becoming evident that only a general reform in the whole diocese would solve our enormous problems.

In January 1986 the twelve priests wrote a harsh letter to the bishop, saying they were tired of fooling themselves about the problems. "We are putting our heads in the sand while our backs are naked, and people are mocking us. It is impossible to continue like this." They requested a formal meeting with the bishop, and it was granted.

Abuna Faraj was determined to attend this meeting. He could barely hold up his head and speak, but I knew he wanted to demonstrate to me and to all the priests his full agreement with our call for reform. We drove him to Haifa and then carried him in his wheelchair into the bishop's residence. He was already exhausted when we arrived.

Abuna Ibrahim, too, was in attendance. My friendship with this fine priest from the village of Makar had grown in the fall of 1985.

For more than two hours we talked, pleaded, and argued with the bishop about the need for reforms in the diocese. Finally the hopelessness of it all began to dawn on us.

Faraj could not outshout even one person, let alone fourteen, but he motioned to us that he wished to speak. Hushing everybody, we encouraged the virtually paralyzed man to say what was on his mind.

"Bishop, for two hours we have discussed the reforms with you, imploring you to take a different direction," Faraj said in a muted voice, speaking in short, breathless phrases. "You are a hopeless case. Nothing positive comes out of you. You are like water, with no shape, no color, no taste."

Abuna Faraj panted a few moments to catch his breath. The room was silent except for his quick breathing. The bishop stared at his helpless accuser.

"I would like to tell you, Bishop, that I will never come here again, because you do not represent Christ for me."

I was shaken by Faraj's words. This gentle, kind man who radiated love and compassion had spoken the truth as he saw it, and it was damning.

The meeting was over, and I was experiencing a strange sensation. When I looked at my bishop, I suddenly saw how alone he was, without a friend in the room.

"Let us leave as brothers, at least," he said, smiling, putting his arms out to one dissatisfied priest.

The priest's response was very sharp. "No, do not hug us as Judas hugged Christ. We do not trust you, and we do not see

Christ in your face. You better take your suitcase and go away from here. You do not represent Christ for us anymore."

The bishop approached the other priests, but the response was the same in each case. "No, don't hug me. You are not worthy of that. You are not really the bishop or the representative of Christ."

I knew the abandonment the bishop was feeling. I had experienced such abandonment when I saw the signatures of all the priests, but this man was experiencing the rejection in front of the people themselves. *God, if I were in his place, I would faint and die.*

Then the bishop came to hug me. I took him by his shoulders and said, "Do not forget. You are the bishop of all Galilee. If your head is not strong on your shoulders, you are lost, and you will get us all lost with you." I would not let him embrace me either. I was afraid if he hugged me now, he would go tell others that everything had been resolved between us, when in truth nothing had been done or even promised.

I did not sleep that night. *O God,* I prayed, *after everything that bishop has done to me, I pity him so much. Give him your grace and mercy. Ease his pain. But, Lord, take his blindness away so he can see that the reforms must be made for the health and survival of the Melkite church in Galilee.*

"Welcome to Rome, Father Chacour," the aide from the Vatican said as he carried my luggage into the hotel. "I will return by one o'clock to take you to the meeting." I had been invited to address the Roman Catholic superiors general, who were in charge of the various Catholic orders and religious communities worldwide.

Rome was a stopover on my flight from the United States to Tel Aviv. The journey had been long and tiring, but I was delighted to be returning home. From March to June 1986 I had been a guest lecturer in theology at McCormick Theological Seminary in Chicago and had also traveled in the United States to speak in various cities about the Palestinian-Israeli conflict.

True to his word, the aide returned in the afternoon and took me to a very large hall where about 450 superiors general and their attendants were gathered.

"Many of you know about the shame in the Holy Land, the care given to the shrines and church buildings," I said. "Our Roman Catholic church spends much time and money on the upkeep of the stones in these places, and many priests, church officials, and tourists visit, focusing their attention upon the buildings.

"I am a priest, a Palestinian from Galilee, and I care about the *true* Custody Terra Sancta, the *living* stones of that land, the people. We must care much more for the living stones that are crying out than for the lifeless antiquities. These living stones are God's children, made in God's image and likeness. Furthermore, the church buildings and the holy shrines are of no value if there is not a living Christian witness in the land to tell what happened with Jesus Christ and what is happening still.

"We Christians, we living stones in the Holy Land, often feel we do not exist in your eyes, you who focus so completely on the lifeless sand and stones of the shrines. What a scandal this is! Our Lord Jesus Christ, born in Galilee, showed us over and over again how much God loves human beings, even giving his life to save them! Aren't we concerned for a real dialogue with our Jewish brothers and sisters to establish more justice on sociopolitical grounds?"

Then I began to speak about the corruption of the churches in the reformed, re-reformed, and not-yet-reformed Christianity of the Holy Land. "One of our biggest problems, the thing I deplore so greatly, is that all but a very few of the men in the Christian hierarchy in the Holy Land are foreigners. This includes all the Christian churches. A Lebanese, a Syrian, an Italian, a German, an American, or a Greek bishop might be very nice, but he cannot feel with or have the sensitivity for the Palestinian parishioners and village priests. He cannot adopt our pain, our hopes, our dreams. We need Palestinian bishops." I then began challenging the superiors general to take seriously the words of Jesus in the Sermon on the Mount, beginning with the Beatitudes.

My passion and enthusiasm were mounting, and a certain cardinal became upset with my message. He stood, magnificent in his red robe, and spoke in a loud, towering voice. "Father Chacour, I want to interrupt you and to ask whether, yes or no, you are in communion with Rome."

The whole group of superiors general froze. What would the Palestinian Greek Catholic priest say in response to the Roman Catholic cardinal?

"Your Eminence," I replied, enunciating my words very carefully in English, "you are a prince of the holy church of God and do not yet know that I am *not* in communion with Rome? It is rather Rome who is in communion with me! Nothing began in Rome. Everything began in Galilee. I want you to know, Eminence, that the pope is sitting over there in that high building because of me. I am not here because of the pope. We in Galilee believed what happened in our streets and our villages, and we came to Rome to tell you about Jesus Christ, to give you the message, to give you Christ himself.

"Since we entrusted you with the Man and his message, Eminence, am I not entitled to ask you, 'What have you done with our Jesus Christ in the big, holy church of God, the Roman Catholic church? Did you reduce him to a theological system? Did you impoverish him to be a set of Christian concepts, a dogma, a theology, a civilization? What has become of my Compatriot in Rome?' You are in communion with me, Eminence, and that is why I can say, yes, I am in communion with you."

The superiors general then began to applaud my words so loudly the cardinal was forced to sit down. I did not intend to embarrass or hurt him, but I needed to say the truth. My words appeared in the Vatican newspaper the following day.

The plane landed in Tel Aviv and taxied a long way before coming to a stop. As usual, the passengers deplaned directly onto the tarmac and walked to the buses that took them to the arrival terminal. And, as usual, the security police were waiting to separate Palestinians from the rest of the travelers.

An officer saw me coming down the stairs and motioned me over to the security van. The police confiscated my passport and took me in the van to the arrival terminal, instructing me to collect my luggage and then go to the "special room" for investigation.

I am very familiar with the special room, having had to visit it every time I have returned to Israel, as has every Palestinian who has entered the country. The room is gloomy and dark, lit only by a weak ceiling light. A table and six or eight chairs are the only furnishings.

"You come with me," a young policeman ordered. I followed him out of the room and into a small cell next door. He searched me thoroughly, then gave another order. "Take off your shoes."

"No, I do not want to take off my shoes," I said, deciding I would preserve my dignity by drawing the line somewhere, even if it just involved my feet and shoes.

"Then you must go back into the room and wait."

"Fine." I sat down to read my book. This time I had chosen to bring *The Diary of Anne Frank*.

Fifteen minutes later the policeman returned. "Are you ready?"

"Yes. Ready for what?"

"Take off your shoes."

"No."

The policeman looked exasperated and I turned back to my book. "What are you reading?" he asked.

"I am reading my own story." I continued reading, turning a page.

"What do you mean?"

"The story of every Palestinian girl is like the story of Anne Frank, but Anne Frank was able to write. Our girls are not yet able to put that into writing, but it is the same treatment you are imposing on us."

"But all I want to do is take your shoes and examine them."

"You will have them under one condition," I said. "You give me a paper and a pen. I want to write a complaint."

"Against whom?"

"Against you. I want to give it to your boss."

"Well, you will have to wait a long time before you get that."

"Fine. I am very busy reading my book." I was well past the point of caring how long this charade would take.

175

After a time the policeman again returned. "Are you ready?"

"No, I want your boss now. Without your boss I will not move from here."

Oppressed people often find measures of freedom and satisfaction in seemingly small, insignificant things. In asserting my right to choose whom I would talk to and whether I would move out of the room willingly, I no longer felt like a prisoner. Now it was the policeman's problem.

"I have plenty of time," I said. "I want to finish this book."

Finally the officer brought his superior, an older, balding man.

"What is it you want?" the senior official demanded.

"This man wants my shoes, but I want a paper and a pen to write a complaint against you. When I have done that, you will have my shoes."

"Bring the paper and pen," the superior ordered.

Putting my book aside, I wrote the following words: "I am so sad that the Israeli authorities are afraid of my shoes. I feel even sadder to see that Israel provides five police officers for every Palestinian who comes through the airport. You will finish by not finding enough police to watch the Palestinians. If you really want peace and security, you will rather order every police officer in the airport to win the friendship of five Palestinians and you will be safe, loved, and respected." I signed the paper and handed it to the official.

He read it, stared at me for a few moments, and then slapped my passport on the table. "We do not want your shoes. Just disappear from here."

"Thank you, sir." I slipped my book and passport into my briefcase, collected my luggage, and left.

In December 1986 I traveled to Houston, Texas, to receive a peace award with my Palestinian lawyer friends, Rajah Shehadeh and Jonathan Kuttab, both from the West Bank. They were being recognized for establishing the human rights organization, Law in the Service of Man in Ramallah and for helping individuals seek justice while under the Israeli military occupation. My own recognition was for the schools and libraries I had built in Galilee, the children's summer camps, and various peace seminars attended by Jewish and Palestinian students through Prophet Elias High School. I received an award from Mrs. Dominique de Menil in Rothko Chapel. The mayor of Houston, Kathryn Whitmire, declared December 11, 1986, a day of solidarity with Palestinians and a day of appreciation for the three of us who had made efforts to establish cooperative, nonviolent alternatives to the Palestinian-Israeli conflict.

On that occasion I was privileged to eat and visit with former U.S. President Jimmy Carter and Archbishop Desmond Tutu, the Nobel Prize–winning Anglican priest from South Africa, who would speak the following day.

"Father Chacour," the archbishop said during dinner, "from what you have told me, there are ways in which your situation in Israel is worse than ours in South Africa."

"Why? What makes you say that?"

"In South Africa, blacks are underprivileged. The whites reserve the privileges to themselves as a matter of deliberate policy and we blacks have the status of second-class citizens. But the whites need our labor. In your situation, it seems Jewish Israelis regard you as dispensable and want you out of the country, wherever you might go."

Jimmy Carter was also concerned about the Palestinian situation. "Father Chacour, what can I do for you?" he asked.

"President Carter, do you have easy access to the White House?"

"Yes, relatively easy."

"Well, then, why don't you meet with President Reagan and tell him to stop shipping weapons and dollars to the Middle East? If he has some sort of sickness that compels him to ship something, please ask him to send Israel thousands of copies of your Constitution so we can learn to live in a democratic, pluralistic, and human society."

Later in the conversation I asked the former president a question that had been troubling me. "President Carter, you are now very outspoken for the Palestinians. Why were you not that outspoken when you had the presidential authority in your hands?"

"I spoke out for a Palestinian homeland during my second month in the White House. Also, the Camp David Accords provide a transitional framework. Now I am much more free when I go to the Middle East to meet and get to know the Palestinians and their plight."

"I hope that you will keep your courage to speak out," I said.

Chapter 22

Crucified in Gaza

Crackling and crashing noises in the garden behind the Peace Center awakened me. It was five o'clock on a summer morning in 1987, and the black goats had returned.

Pulling on my clothes and shoes, I hurried out to my beloved garden. We had carved a flat area out of the hillside and hauled in rich, dark soil, creating a perfect place to grow fruit trees, vines, vegetables, and flowers. Every morning and evening I visited my citrus and olive trees, watering them, examining them, talking to them. Sometimes I even pulled on them a little to encourage them to grow. The trees were like my children.

Black goats will go anywhere to find food, even trying to climb trees. Our neighbor near the Peace Center owned black goats, and my garden frequently had been victimized by their early morning marauding. Soon after I planted tender young trees, I would discover they had been devoured.

Quietly I approached one small goat who was busy chewing on a tree. Grabbing it by the horns, I shouted, "Get out of here! Get out!" The other goats ran, but I had my prisoner firmly in hand. The goat screamed and resisted my efforts as I pulled it through the end room of the Peace Center and down the two outside flights of stairs to the parking lot below.

Margie and Tony Sullivan, guests from Michigan, appeared on the balcony in their bathrobes. They watched in amazement as I imprisoned the goat in a storage space beneath the stairs, penning it in with cinder blocks. I brought water and bread, but the goat only continued screaming.

"Abuna, what on earth is going on?" Margie Sullivan called.

"This goat and its relatives have eaten my trees time and again. Now I am taking this goat as a hostage," I said, joining them on the balcony.

"A hostage? You've taken a *goat* hostage?" Tony was incredulous.

"You have a right to be upset, but why punish this one particular goat? Is it guilty?" Margie was not sure whether to be serious or humorous.

"No more than the police dog who bites at the order of a police officer," I replied, "but what about me? Am I guilty for protecting my trees? The goats do not know any better, but the owner will understand. She lets her goats run wild, so I have imprisoned one until she comes."

Within an hour Abuna Awad, the village chairman, the directors of all the schools, and assorted friends and relatives had received early-morning telephone calls from the goat owner. "Come and see!" the woman cried. "Abuna Elias took my goat as a hostage, and he will give the goat to the police. My goat will die, because the police have no way to care for it. Please intervene to liberate my goat!"

At eight o'clock Abuna Awad and another man came to negotiate for the goat's liberation. The animal was still screaming underneath the stairs.

"Abuna Elias, what is going on? Why have you taken this goat hostage?" Abuna Awad could not stop laughing.

I, in all seriousness, told them my story about the numerous times the goats had eaten my trees. "Go and bring me the amount of money I paid for my trees or bring me new trees, and I will liberate the goat."

Still laughing, Abuna Awad left.

"The goat owner is calling everyone she knows to call me names and make all sorts of accusations," I told the Sullivans and others who had now gathered. "I am the one who has lost trees and money, yet I'm the one being maligned. They want the goat liberated, but in truth I am the one who will be released when it's over."

"What will happen now, Abuna?" Margie asked.

"Now they will probably try to free the goat by a trick or military operation," I predicted. Sure enough, we soon spotted the twelve-year-old son of the goat owner, creeping on his hands and knees down the hill. When he reached the goat, he carefully removed the cinder blocks.

"What are you doing there?" I shouted, and the boy ran away. The hostage goat was free and had stopped screaming, but did not leave.

"Maybe this is the hostage syndrome," I laughed. "Perhaps the goat feels happier here than at home now."

Later in the morning the goat owner came to negotiate, and we agreed on a plan. She would keep her goats out of my garden and pay me for my trees when she had the funds. Although I knew I would never see the money, I released my hostage. The goat screamed and screamed as the owner led it away.

As we ate lunch, the Sullivans, some other guests, and I discussed the morning's events.

"This has turned out to be a perfect example of what the world calls terrorism, the mix-up of so many evils, piled one on top of the other," I said. "Think about it. Who was the real terrorist here? Me, the goats, or the goat owner?"

"The goat owner," several people agreed.

"Exactly. She cared nothing about me or my garden but simply did what she wanted, allowing her goats to roam and eat without supervision.

"Both the garden and the captured goat were victims. The garden was almost destroyed, and the poor goat was the frightened hostage. I was the one who was terrorized, fearing daily for my garden. Then my reputation was damaged by the real terrorist. Everyone saw *me* as the terrorist, although I had been the one terrorized all along.

"It really is not right to accuse those who take hostages of being terrorists. Of course I am not justifying hostage taking, but too often we who observe these events think only about politics and the immediate problem. We ignore or overlook the history and the reality of the situation, which always involves an oppression of some group of people. Anytime we corner the oppressed in a situation of despair and hopelessness, we are forcing them to kick back with our own rejective methods. As you observed today, the so-called terrorist may very well be the terrorized one. Go and apply that to the Palestinians, please."

In September 1987 Rabbi Meir Kahane and his friends stormed into Biram, sending terror into the hearts of the former residents and their children. Rabbi Kahane and the Israeli political party Kach, which he heads, are well known for their extremist, racist views and actions against Arab Palestinian people in Israel and Occupied Palestine. Rabbi Kahane and Kach see the expulsion of Arab Palestinians from all of Israel, the West Bank, and Gaza as the solution to the "Arab problem," keeping Eretz Yisrael, Greater Israel, only for Jewish people.[1] Rabbi Kahane won election to the Knesset on this platform in 1984. Therefore, in 1987 he had protection from prosecution for his actions.

During their rampage, Rabbi Kahane and his gang wrote messages on the wall of Biram's church, saying, "We shall teach you, people of Biram, you have no right to return." They destroyed all the crosses that were carved on the archways and doorways of still partially standing houses. The crosses on the church had already been obliterated. Under the protection of the police, Rabbi Kahane and his people brought a bulldozer and demolished the work the residents of Biram had done during their work camps, including the partially rebuilt school. Also destroyed in the melee was the dirt walkway through the trees to the church. The children of the 1987 Biram summer camp had painstakingly swept the path and lined it with small pebbles.

Rabbi Kahane's attack also tore down the fragile hope and confidence the people of Biram were beginning to feel. Undoubtedly the attack was intended to do just that. Writing slogans, defacing buildings, and bulldozing a partially rebuilt school are silly acts, ineffectual in and of themselves. They are intended to convey a larger message about who is the master and who is the unwanted slave.

We will continue to rebuild our village. Furthermore, we shall never leave, even if extremists try to kill us. If they kill us, then we will stay here forever, buried in our beloved land.

We do not want the Jews to leave either, even those who have recently come from Europe, the Soviet Union, and the United States. We want them to stay with us in our homeland, enjoying the beauty of Palestine. How can we be selfish when we love Palestine? We can only share our love so our love can endure.

"Khader took his bicycle and went out to get some fruit and bread for the family, Abuna. When he found the stores were closed, he went to visit some friends in the Old City of Gaza where we used to live. People said the stores might open in the afternoon."

Khader's mother was surrounded by relatives and friends in her living room as she told her story. My heart was sick because I already knew the ending of this story. Khader Elias Tarazi, age nineteen, had been killed on February 8, declared dead on February 9, and buried on February 10, 1988.[2] He was the first Christian martyr in the Gaza Strip during *Intifada*.

In December 1987 the struggle for freedom known as *Intifada* had begun in the West Bank and the Gaza Strip, areas of the original Palestine that had been under Israeli military occupation since 1967.

Intifada is an Arabic word that literally means "shaking off," getting rid of something unwanted. In the Gospels we hear Jesus tell his disciples to "shake off" the dust from their feet if a household or village does not accept them or their teachings. In the media, *Intifada* is often defined as "uprising" or "rebellion." The true definition of "shaking off" is much more applicable to what is happening in the West Bank and Gaza. After more than twenty years of Israeli military occupation, the 1.5 million Palestinians living in those territories are saying to Israel, "Enough! We do not agree to be occupied anymore. We have lost not only our land, homes, work, and families, but also our dignity and our future. We are going to 'shake off' this occupation, letting you and the whole world know that we want our freedom."

Children born and raised during the occupation are taking the lead. Using the land itself to express their indignation and their refusal to accept the status quo, the young people throw stones at the unwanted, unwelcome Israeli soldiers armed with sophisticated weaponry. Claiming their lives are in danger, the soldiers shoot and beat the young people. Hundreds of Palestinians have been killed, thousands wounded, and tens of thousands imprisoned.

Khader Tarazi had graduated from secondary school and was trying to decide what his next step would be. He could stay at home and work in his father's jewelry business, learning the trade, or he could go to a university. Either way, the economic situation was bleak. Like that of every other Palestinian teenager living under occupation, his whole future was bleak.

In March 1988, three months after *Intifada* began, I was invited to go to the Gaza Strip with a small group of observers from the Pontifical Mission in Jerusalem. Our purpose was to visit people called the Families of Martyrs and to bring them relief supplies, to hear their stories, and most important, give them our human presence, care, and comfort.

The Gaza Strip is about forty-five kilometers long and eight kilometers wide (twenty-eight by five miles). This area was artificially created in 1948 and was under Egyptian control until 1967. The Gaza Strip and the West Bank were then taken under Israeli military control but never annexed, only occupied. The people have no civil rights yet they must pay taxes. Until *Intifada*, the Palestinian people in the Occupied Territories literally paid the cost of their own occupation.[3] Now taxes are being withheld and other nonviolent protests are being employed.

The Gaza Strip is one of the most densely populated areas in the world, with well over 600,000 Palestinian people jammed into the small space.[4] About 70 percent of the people are refugees, the majority of whom live in eight refugee camps. As in Galilee, about 50 percent of the people are fourteen years of age or younger, meaning they have known no other life than the hated Israeli military occupation.[5]

Driving along the main road, we entered Gaza City. This was not a curfew or strike day, so people were out purchasing food and supplies while they could. Soldiers, jeeps, Uzi submachine guns, tanks, and tear gas guns and cannisters were everywhere. I was chilled by the militarism and the fear.

We spent the day visiting in the homes of six families. Each family had a martyr, a child or teenager who had been killed. All were anxious to tell their stories. It was one of the most agonizing days of my life, because I was hearing, seeing, and touching people who were in such deep anguish. Through them I experienced the pain myself, weeping with them in their tremendous loss. Despite the pain, or perhaps because of the pain, each family was determined that the occupation must end and saw *Intifada* as the way to accomplish that.

In the early afternoon we came to the Tarazi home. The house was in Gaza City, not in a refugee camp, because the Tarazi family was originally from Gaza. They are Roman Catholic Christians, one of only a few Christian families left in Gaza. The father and mother welcomed us to their home and served us coffee and fruit.

Khader's mother, a university graduate, told her son's story, showing us his picture.

Khader, while visiting his old neighborhood, had suddenly found himself in the middle of a skirmish between Israeli soldiers and young Palestinians. Witnesses later told Khader's parents that their son had not thrown stones but had run to get away from the trouble. He fled into the familiar house of Um Issam, a family friend, and she hid him under her bed. Four soldiers smashed the door and searched the house, finding Khader under the bed. They beat him with clubs and with the butts of their guns. Um Issam, about sixty-five years old, screamed and tried to help the young man, but she, too, was beaten and severely injured.

One of the soldiers, apparently crazy with rage, lifted Khader over his head and slammed his body to the cement floor. According to Um Issam, Khader then lay motionless, blood pouring from his mouth and eyes, while yet another soldier kicked him in the genitals.

Khader then was dragged out of the house and thrown face down on the hood of the jeep, his head hanging down over the front and his feet straight back toward the windshield. His arms were stretched outward and tied down in a crucifixion position. The soldiers then began beating him again, witnessed by scores of people who had now gathered. Blood gushed from his mouth and nose, running down the front of the jeep. At this point he probably was dead. The soldiers then drove away with the young man still tied to the front of the jeep.

Apparently the soldiers drove with Khader on the jeep for a long time, periodically beating him. The parents, having been notified by friends and relatives, tried to locate their son, contacting the Red Cross and the United Nations representatives in Gaza, and visiting police and detention centers. The only information they were given was that Khader was being "detained."

On Tuesday morning, February 9, a Tarazi relative was told by an Israeli military officer that Khader was dead, but no further information was given. The immediate family was not officially notified. The parents went to the Israeli military headquarters to inquire about the location of Khader's body. After a very long wait, an officer said that Khader had died of a "heart attack," and his body was at a government hospital in Beersheba, about fifty kilometers away inside Israel. Now all the family wanted was to hold a Christian funeral and decently bury their son.

On Wednesday afternoon, February 10, people began gathering at the Latin Catholic church for the funeral, but the military delayed release of Khader's body. When the body finally arrived, a Tarazi relative who is a doctor in a Gaza hospital examined it. Khader's back was broken, his right front skull fractured, bones in each arm and the right hand broken, and there were multiple lacerations all over the body. Internal injuries could not be determined. An autopsy obviously had been done, the long abdominal-chest wound having been stitched up. In addition, there were curious slits up the fronts of his legs, which had been crudely stitched closed. The doctor took a photograph of the mutilated body.

Despite the delays, more than six hundred people were still gathered at the church. Although the military promised the family it would stay away, allowing the funeral to proceed, there was a massive deployment of soldiers, and angry confrontations between mourners and soldiers occurred. While prayers and singing went on in the church, tear gas bombs were fired into the church courtyard, where many people were standing.

The funeral procession was allowed to move from the church to the cemetery, the casket draped with the Palestinian flag. Khader's picture and other smaller flags were displayed. In the cemetery, during the prayers of committal, more tear gas was fired into the crowd of about 350 mourners gathered around the grave, forcing everyone to scatter. The priest finally laid Khader's body to rest.[6]

That afternoon I wept and prayed with the Tarazi family, holding them very close. Outside in the streets of Gaza normal activities were taking place. This was a relatively good day and despite *Intifada* and the occupation, people were going about the business of living.

When I returned to Ibillin, I felt torn in two directions. Part of me wanted to tell everyone about the atrocities in Gaza, but another part of me said, "Be very careful! You could fan the flames of hatred." I prayed for a long time in the grotto, asking God for wisdom.

I remembered the experience with Rabbi Sugarman and his congregation in Atlanta, Georgia. He had invited me to speak in the synagogue, and about eight hundred Jewish people listened to me for two hours. I told them that in the eyes of Palestinians in the refugee camps and in the villages of the Occupied Territories, Jews are not decent, civilized, or educated people. They are soldiers or occupiers or terrorists. "That is the image our children have of you," I told the people in Atlanta. "Our task is to rehumanize ourselves in each other's eyes."

Toward the end of my speech I told my Jewish audience that I did not have a "nice dream" to solve all this. Rather, we people from Galilee have visions, and we believe our visions will become reality.

I explained, "I have a vision of two children, a Jew and a Palestinian, who are friends. One day these children celebrate their friendship. The Palestinian child brings an Israeli flag for his brother, and the Jewish child brings his Palestinian brother a handmade Palestinian flag. They hug each other and say, 'We were so ignorant, so blind, to believe that those who gave us money and weapons were our friends. They were our enemies. They used and abused us.'"

Rabbi Sugarman came to me in front of his congregation with tears in his eyes. For the first time he called me Abuna.

"Abuna, would you please give me your blessing in front of my community?" He turned to his congregation, saying, "If anyone is angry, the door is open and you can leave."

I put my hand on his head and gave him the blessing in Hebrew.

"I will not become your brother," Rabbi Sugarman said to me following the blessing. "I have discovered I already *was* your brother, and we did not know each other."

Violence begets violence. The cycle must be broken. I cannot react to violence with another bigger or smaller violence, and I must not encourage or enable others to do so either. In the face of violence, we must try to be genuine, creative, disarming. This is extremely difficult. We might be killed, but then we will know that we have chosen between a long, empty life and a short, full one. It is far better to get our hands dirty building a human society than to complacently keep our hands clean.

Soft cooing and singing sometimes awaken me early in the morning. Instead of black goats, I am visited by thirty or forty pairs of pheasants who dance, sing, and eat near my bedroom window at the Peace Center. It is so beautiful. My trees are growing tall and the garden is lush with food, flowers, and vines. The cries of the terrorized were heard, adjustments were made, and now all live in peace and tranquility.

Chapter 23

No More Dirty Anybody!

"There is no file, Father Chacour, because you did not apply for a building permit." The supervisor of the Ministry of Interior Affairs spoke firmly to me and my Jewish friend. We had come to Akko in May 1988 to inquire about the permit for the new gymnasium, library, and technology classroom building, which was already under construction.

"Of course I did! I applied over a year ago and have been telephoning periodically to check on the application. Someone always says, 'We are studying your application,' but no one ever does anything about it."

"There is no file," the man repeated. "That means you did not apply."

"I can prove I applied." Opening my briefcase, I pulled out the receipt issued a year earlier, acknowledging my application.

The supervisor turned red as he examined the receipt. Then he shouted at his assistant. "I never saw this file! Where the hell is it? Find it!"

The file was nowhere to be found, so we were asked to return the following day.

When my friend and I arrived the next morning, the supervisor had the proper file on his desk. "It was way at the back of a drawer in the outer office," he said. "We had received orders to put the file aside and not deal with it."

I was infuriated that we had been cast aside for a whole year. "We will take this to court, and my friend here will help us!"

"Now, Father Chacour, do not be hasty. If you sue, you will hurt your own bishop, because he is the one who instructed us through the government official not to deal with your project."

I stared at the supervisor and then at my friend, nodding my head. *I should have known,* I thought. *I should have known.*

We had applied for the new permit in April 1987 and had begun construction in the summer. Jim and Linda Ryan from Maryland had encouraged us with their generous financial gifts and their loving support. Located just below the road leading up to the high school, the ground-level classrooms were nearly completed, and the gymnasium on the second level was taking shape. There had been no interference from the police during this construction, which had been contracted out to local builders. Everything was going smoothly. Until now.

"Brother, can you come home right away?" Atallah telephoned me in the United States where I was on a speaking tour in Ohio during October 1988. "Father doesn't know us, and he's behaving strangely. Maybe he will die."

Within two days I had arrived in Haifa, joining my frightened family. Father, who had been in good health and had had a perfect memory even at the age of ninety, had suddenly collapsed mentally.

"Hello, Father," I said, joining him as he sat on his daybed in Atallah's living room. "I have come to visit you." At first I thought Father recognized me, but then realized he only saw a priest in a cassock.

"You are a priest, the representative of God. Take me from this prison, I beg of you. These soldiers we received so well—they will kill our children who are our wealth, our treasure. God has entrusted our children to us. Please, please, you must help me," Father implored. The kind, gentle face I knew so well was twisted with fear and intense suffering. His pain was so consuming, so real, that I, too, experienced his agony.

I gathered him in my arms, trying to comfort him. "Father, you are not in prison. You are here in Atallah's house, in your bed. I am your priest son, and I love you. Please don't be afraid. Everyone is safe."

But Father could not hear me. The fear had taken over his mind, his memory, his senses, and his frail body.

In October and November 1948 Father had been thrown out of his village, loaded like cattle into a truck with his three oldest sons, and then thrown out of his country while the rest of his family fended for themselves. Exactly forty years later, something triggered the cruel memories, and Father was back in 1948. He relived every detail of his expulsion, beginning with the meeting of the village elders in which it had been decided to welcome the Jewish Zionist soldiers into the village.

In Atallah's living room, Father spoke to the phantom elders. "We will receive the soldiers well, because they are our co-persecuted brothers and sisters. We must show them through our actions that a persecuted people can welcome another persecuted people." Father was referring to the severe oppressions the Palestinians had suffered while under five centuries of Turkish occupation, which had ended only in 1917. "That's settled then! We will slaughter lambs when our guests arrive, and we will celebrate their liberation with a great feast!"

Suddenly Father's mood changed radically. He stood up and addressed Rudah, whom he seemed to think was the commanding military officer. "I don't understand. Why must we leave our houses? Your soldiers are comfortable inside our homes. We are sleeping on the roofs, and we are cooking their food. We are happy to do that until it is time for you to leave."

Rudah tried to calm him, but Father did not hear. "You think this village is in danger of being attacked? By whom?" We were quiet, hardly breathing. Father was totally involved in acting out his story.

"Perhaps you are right. Our families would be safer outside the village if there's an attack. Yes, we will leave our belongings here in your care along with the keys to the houses. You have given us a paper promising our return in two weeks so we will leave immediately."

My brothers, sister, and I remembered the days spent under the olive trees and in grottoes. Now Father was describing the experience from a parent's point of view.

"Katuub, we must keep the children warm. Here, hold Elias and Atallah close to you, and Wardi, too. The rest of us will encircle you, and we can be very close. Just a few more days and we can be back in our warm house, children."

We heard about the struggle to find food, about our parents' fears for the lives of us children, about how the old people had suffered, and about the conferences among the elders as the days had dragged on and on.

At one point Father described the men's effort to infiltrate the village secretly in order to get warm dress and food for their children. The soldiers had chased them and they had barely escaped. After that the elders had known something was drastically wrong. They had faced the soldiers with the signed paper, demanding the right to return to Biram, but there would be no return. The paper and the promise were meaningless.

"*You!*" Father shouted, pointing at poor Rudah. "You were the officer who gave us the written promise! You *lied* to us! And you mocked us when we saw how you ransacked our houses and ruined our belongings."

Suddenly Father was in prison again. He turned to me, the priest. "My dear priest," he implored, "please take me away from this prison. This officer cheated us, and he will kill us all now as I saw them killing so many innocent young boys in Jish. Please, I just want my family to be safe. I don't care about land or houses."

Father, so frightened, wept in my arms. The whole family wept as we sat together in the house in Haifa. It was 1948 again, and our family was suffering just outside Biram.

In November Father began speaking of his deportation. When the villagers had discovered the terrible deception, the soldiers had prevented their return. At gunpoint, Father, Rudah, Chacour, Mousa, and the other men from Biram had been loaded into military trucks. While the rest of us were left to wander outside the village, the men had been driven to the border and forced to cross into the West Bank. The soldiers had threatened them with death if they returned, firing guns over their heads to make them run faster. At ninety years of age, Father was once again escaping the gunfire, trying to protect his sons, making sure they stayed together. He was trembling with fear.

For several weeks we watched Father as he reexperienced the agonies and hardships of being an unwanted refugee in Jordan, Syria, and Lebanon. He and the boys had kept moving, hoping to find their way back to Biram, to their family. He recounted their miseries in vivid detail. Father was longing for his wife and children, for his fig trees and olive trees. "I am angry with you, beloved God," he wept. "Why is all this inflicted on us? Do something!" Father pleaded over and over.

"Why won't our Arab brothers and sisters help us?" he cried a few moments later. "They act as if we are cowards, people to be ignored or even chased away. Don't they know we were forced to leave our homes? Can't they imagine that we are hungry? Can't they see that our clothes are falling off us, and our shoes are in ribbons?"

Father wandered around and around the room, as if he were making the journey once again. He was working so hard and no matter what we said or did, he ignored us.

Refugees are uncared for, unprotected, voiceless people. Because they have no money, they are usually regarded as worthless themselves. They are despised and easily labeled "dirty terrorists." Father and the boys had struggled as wandering refugees for almost three months. They had found some respite in Lebanon, it seemed, where many Palestinian refugees had fled.

One day in early December I sat with Father in the evening. Suddenly he whispered, "My sons! Come! Come! It's time to cross the border." Father then began describing how he and his sons, terrified and terrorized, had managed to cross the Lebanon-Israel border under cover of darkness. They were headed for Biram, the goal of their long, excruciating journey.

Atallah telephoned me the next day. "You better come, Brother. Father is close to Biram. He is so weak but very excited. I don't know what's going to happen when he discovers the empty village."

"I'm on my way," I replied.

Atallah was right. Father was reaching the climax of his journey, and when it finally ended there would probably be a big change in his condition. He might die. Or he might live the experience over and over. No matter what happened, I wanted to be with him.

Atallah met me at the door. "He's in Biram. They're walking around and around, looking at everything."

When I entered the living room, Father was pacing, poking at things with his walking stick. "See that, Chacour? All the grain, all the figs, all the wheat has been dumped out and scattered everywhere. It's not fit to eat. And the olive oil—look! What a terrible, terrible waste! It's been poured over everything. All that precious oil, a whole year's supply!"

Father stopped his rummaging. He looked into the distance and announced, "I heard they might be in Jish. We will go there."

Seated once again on the daybed, Father spoke with a shepherd from Jish who had come by with his flock early in the morning. Yes, the shepherd had said, the people of Biram were in Jish, those who did not go to Lebanon.

After entering Jish in his imagination, Father inquired in a whisper, "Where is the family of Mikhail Chacour? Where is the woman Um Rudah, wife of Mikhail?"

I was sitting closer to Father on the daybed. We were coming to the climax of the story. Father was totally engrossed in his experience.

He tapped the walking stick on the floor. "I am knocking on the door. 'Who is there?' calls Katuub. 'I am Mikhail,' I reply. But she doesn't believe me. She can't believe me. She is convinced I am dead. Now the door is opening." Father was sobbing. "I see my wife. She sees me."

I held Father very close and sobbed with him. My brothers and sister gathered around and hugged us both.

For two hours Father cried in my arms. All the grief and pain, sorrow and loss poured out of him. When he was quiet, I helped him lie down. His eyes were closed, and he seemed to be asleep. Just as I was about to leave, Father opened his eyes. They were clear. He looked directly at me. "Hello, my son," he said.

The three-month-long drama was over. Soon Father acted and spoke normally, but he had lost most of his physical strength.

Watching Father relive his horrendous experience made me wonder what is happening to the hearts and minds of all the people in Occupied Palestine who are systematically being harassed, injured, tortured, and mutilated by the Jewish Israeli soldiers. If my father at the age of ninety could be so deeply affected by a tragedy that occurred forty years ago, what will the Palestinian children and young people of today be feeling and thinking twenty, thirty, forty years from now? What will they tell their children to do? Will they all be like my father, who repeatedly said to his children, "Do not do like the Jewish soldiers do to you. This is evil. God neither persecutes nor tortures people, God does not hate the poor, and God does not kill. God loves us. God is with the oppressed, suffers with them, and sides with them for liberation."

What is happening to the hearts and minds of the Jewish soldiers who are acting in such inhuman ways? In the future will they see themselves as responsible for deaths and injuries? Will they blame their superiors? Will they claim that "state reasons" were of primary importance? This is frightening and sad. The heart and soul of a people are being destroyed from within by a dangerous combination of fear and arrogance.

How can the injustice against the Palestinian people be repaired? For that matter, how can the injustice done against the Amerindians of North America, the aborigines of Australia, the Armenians, or the Jews in the Second World War ever be repaired? With money? With vengeance? With efforts to replace or duplicate the situation before the injustice? The truth is that the horrors that have been done are beyond repair. We must remember these horrors and be outraged enough to declare, "No more slaughters! No more genocide! No more concentration camps! No more dirty Indians, aborigines, Armenians, or Jews! In fact, no more dirty *anybody!*"

The Palestinian injustice, like others in the world, is now in process. Do we have the courage to recognize that the Palestinians suffer as the victims of the children of the concentration camp martyrs? If not directly, at least they are the victims of a post-Holocaust mentality in the Jewish world and the Western Christian world. What repair, what adjustments, can be made to stop the injustice and allow a new beginning?

Some sought repair by telling the Jewish Israelis to leave this country so it can once again be Palestine. Such an idea is wrong and not at all feasible. Israel exists as a state and it will continue to exist. The injustice against the Palestinians cannot be repaired by creating a bigger injustice. However, the quality of Israel's existence needs to be questioned. The recognition of Israel's right to exist does not support or condone its continued development at the expense of the Palestinians.

Imagine that you have destroyed my house. Would destroying your house and family be the answer to this injustice? Or is the answer to ask you to contribute to the building of another house for me and my family? Many Jews, Palestinians, and other concerned people believe that the only feasible and thinkable solution is to create a Palestinian state on a part of the original Palestine, existing side by side with Israel. In other words, the destroyed Palestinian house must be rebuilt without destroying the Israeli house in the process. The good solution to a problem is one in which both sides make concessions, sometimes large ones, saying, "We did not get everything we wanted, but we got some of what we wanted." A solution in which one side is happy and the other unhappy only lays the foundation for a bigger explosion in the future.

We Palestinians and Jews live in what the world calls the Holy Land, but what makes the land holy? Is it the stones or trees? Is it the churches? The shrines? The paths on which the patriarchs and our Lord Jesus Christ walked? Or is the land sanctified by what we *do* to make God present?

"Father is dying," Atallah told me on the telephone. "The doctor says he will not live much longer." Once again I hurried home from the United States, where I had been speaking in April 1989.

Father is living yet, but not in his beloved Galilee. Instead he is with the God who chose Galilee as his own home on this earth and assured us, "When I am lifted up, I shall lift you up with me."

I was able to spend one week by Father's bedside before his frail body exhausted itself. The funeral was held in the Melkite church in Haifa, where many priests, family members, and friends gathered to praise God for the life of Mikhail Chacour. Then the people rode on a bus to Biram, accompanying us as we took Father's body to be buried next to Katuub, my mother. Father had finally returned to Biram.

Chapter 24

Dry Bones Will Come
Back to Life

I had come to hate the sight of the new school building. There it stood on the side of the hill, a partially clad skeleton, abandoned by its architects and builders. It was a constant reminder of the unfinished task, the tremendous need of the Palestinian students in Galilee, and my own feelings of frustration and failure.

A court order had stopped construction in September 1988. By that time we had completed the ground floor with several large classrooms, as well as three-quarters of the gymnasium on the second level. Because we did not have a building permit, the order stated, all work must cease, and anyone found working on the building would be imprisoned. The contractor, architect, and laborers were contacted personally and threatened. There was no choice but to stop the construction.

I was remanded to court for a February 1989 appearance. There I was to defend myself against the state of Israel, which was asking for payment of a large fine and immediate destruction of the building. I would even be required to pay the cost of the demolition. Already over a half-million U.S. dollars had been invested in the extension to the school, money that had come from Jim and Linda Ryan, World Vision International, the Pontifical Mission, Sue Wolfe, and other generous donors. Students were already learning in the ground-floor classrooms.

As soon as the court order stopped the construction, I began storming the gates of the Israeli governmental bureaucracy to shake loose the building permit. Just when the permit was within sight, someone would jerk it away with a crazy objection or request. Once I was told the building was ten meters away from its correct spot. Another time I was instructed to have all new blueprints drawn, because the others were too old. The new blueprints cost nearly one thousand U.S. dollars.

Just before my court date and the municipal elections in Israel, an Orthodox Jewish official in the Ministry of Interior Affairs telephoned me, setting up a meeting on Saturday, the Jewish Sabbath. A Jewish friend accompanied me and together we "heard" the man offer a building permit in exchange for guaranteed votes. Running on the Likud ticket, this man advocated the transfer of Arabs from Akko so the city would be strictly Jewish. No Palestinian Israeli living in Akko would vote for him.

"Heard" is only a figurative term, because once we were in his home, the official refused to speak aloud. Anything he wanted to say, he wrote on small pieces of paper, which he destroyed after I had read them. Apparently he was afraid my friend or I was carrying a tape recorder.

The man showed me official ballots for the election and then wrote, "You will have to take the ballots, which I have marked in my own way. Then you give me the names of your friends, and I will observe you distributing the ballots to them. I will recognize the ballots when they are cast."

I examined them closely and handed them back. "Sir, I respect you as a human being, but I tell you this: even if you come to destroy the school one hundred times, I will not distribute one of these ballots. If you give me the permit tomorrow, however, I will visit some of my friends in Akko and say, 'Rejoice with me. I have the permit.' I will tell them we have it because you were kind, and I will mention your name. More than that you will never get from me." Needless to say, no building permit was issued.

I had no doubt that the bishop had stirred up the difficulties we were experiencing with the elusive building permit and the Israeli orders to stop construction and appear in court. For reasons of his own, he did not want the school extension built. I was determined to overcome these objections and obstacles, finishing the school building for the hundreds of students now depending on us for their education and their future.

"I really miss Faraj," I said to Abuna Ibrahim. We were walking back and forth on the dusty playground just above the unfinished building during the noon break. "I miss going to Nazareth and talking with him. I miss his beautiful smile."

"What do you hear from him? Does he like Australia?"

"I haven't heard anything. All I know is that Ilonka took him to her home and family for one year. She decided she could care for him better there, and he was excited to go."

Students were enjoying their break in the warm June sunshine, eating, laughing, strolling. The sounds of carpentry drifted up to us from the unfinished building. Danny and Phil, two volunteers from the Hutterite community in the United States, had worked hard to clear the cement floor and bleachers in the gymnasium of all the wood, metal, and cinder blocks. Now they were constructing a platform, preparing the open-air shell of a gymnasium for the Prophet Elias High School 1989 graduation ceremony.

"It will be exciting to have the ceremony in the gymnasium," Abuna Ibrahim said as we gazed down at the building. "They might stop us from building, but they cannot stop us from using what we have."

"Unless they demolish it," I reminded him.

"That is not likely to happen. The threat of international publicity is probably enough to keep the bulldozers away, and don't forget, the students and faculty have all said that if the bulldozers arrive, they will sit in the building and refuse to move."

"True, very true," I said. "It will be a memorable evening."

The lunch break was over and we began walking back to the school. "Just imagine, Ibrahim, I have been in this village for nearly twenty-five years. Sometimes I think I will leave, but it is impossible. I belong in Galilee just as Galilee belongs in me. Ibillin has become my home. The people have become my people. Together we have accomplished amazing things."

"God willing, there will be many more. Like a community college, for instance. Isn't that your next dream?"

"Yes, but God's willingness must be matched with our willingness to work and struggle for what we need right in the midst of the situation."

Anticipation, laughter, and excitement filled the air the evening of June 17, 1989. Eighty-six students would soon receive their diplomas from Prophet Elias High School. They were the sixth graduating class in our history, but the first to graduate in the new gymnasium.

The unfinished shell, open to the cool, brisk evening wind, offered stark contrasts to the eye. The silent gray cinder blocks waiting to be used to complete the gymnasium were stacked along the walls, mutely testifying to our delayed dreams and our enormous frustration and pain. A pillar of cinder blocks three or four meters high had been erected on the right side of the wooden platform, a towering declaration of our intention to continue the work of building a hope and future for Palestinian young people in Galilee. Bright school flags hanging from the ragged walls waved in the wind. Yellow, red, blue, and white plastic chairs were arranged in rows. A video camera waited to record this historic occasion.

With deep emotion I watched the crowds of people ascend the Mount of Light and make their way through the construction site to the gymnasium. Twenty Israeli government officials arrived, some from the prime minister's Office for Arab Affairs. They were seated as honored guests in the wide front row. Many heads of local councils were present, representing the villages from which our students come. Parents and family members, numbering well over eight hundred, streamed into the gymnasium. Nearly all the students in the school had come to witness the graduation, dreaming of the day they, too, would complete their work. By the time the program began, fifteen hundred persons filled the gymnasium shell to capacity, and my joy was overflowing. The empty, mournful space had been transformed by the presence and spirit of the living stones.

The graduates entered in a proud, happy procession, filling the seats reserved for them facing the platform on either side.

The young women all wore pink dresses in various styles, and the young men were resplendent in dark suits and pink shirts. It was quite a transformation from the school uniform of blue cotton shirts and blue jeans.

"Welcome to Prophet Elias High School and the graduation ceremony of the class of 1989!" the director of the school announced, calling a guest clergy to bless the crowd with an opening prayer. A singing group from the school entertained, followed by a tumbling team, which laid a few mats on the hard concrete and turned somersaults and flips. They concluded their gymnastic presentation by forming a pyramid, raising the school flag, and releasing a cloud of colored balloons into the fast-darkening Galilee sky. The audience applauded and cheered, and some women were ululating.

I sat in the audience, drinking in the joy and excitement, pushing aside the habitual pain and fatigue. For the first time I was feeling completely justified and vindicated in the decision to build without the permit. We had created a fact on the ground, an already-born baby. The Israeli authorities *must* cope with it, and I felt sure we would eventually receive our permit. If we had waited to build until receiving the permit, we would never have this building.

My address to the graduates and the audience was the last in a series of greetings by Palestinian Israeli dignitaries.

What a sight met my eyes as I stood at the podium! Fifteen hundred of my friends, coworkers, students, and acquaintances were smiling at me and applauding. I could see the faculty and the students, the tiny children and the excited graduates, the proud parents and the slightly uncomfortable Israeli officials. Also visible were the volunteers from all over the world: John and Sandra Lapp, Mennonites from the United States, long-term volunteer teachers and librarians; Marie Nyunt, the French-English speaking secretary World Vision had hired for me in Burma; Hildegard Voss from Denmark, who cared so well for the volunteers; Phil and Danny, Hutterites from the United States. There, too, were Zada, Sister Nazarena, and Sister Gislaine. I felt surrounded by their love and support.

In my address I wanted to invoke God's blessing on the graduates and our school, inject the blood of courage' into students and parents, and send a clear message to the Israeli authorities, some of whom were sitting before me. After much prayer and thought, I had decided to use the text about the dry bones coming to life by the power of God, Ezekiel 37.

"We do not have dry bones all about us. Rather we have scattered cinder blocks, which are useless until they are joined together. Very soon, my friends, these dusty cinder blocks will rise up and begin to take shape. The flesh and sinews of plasterboard, wood, windows, and tiles will cover the skeleton. The life breath will blow when the students are fully utilizing the building.

"This ingathering of people tonight is in anticipation of the role of the unfinished gymnasium. We, the living stones, are forming one body. We are declaring the future. Who can stop the scattered cinder blocks from becoming one building, one strong, useful building?

"We need to tell the Israeli authorities that the extended hand of God will do this. They should not, they must not, become the obstacle but rather remember the story of the dry bones. Ezekiel shouts that when the Word of God goes out, it never returns without accomplishing its mission. That, too, is our cry tonight! These dry bones, these cinder blocks, will rise and come to life, fulfilling their purpose! Our future will be what we want it to be!"

During the intermission in the graduation program, the school singers performed while lemonade and cookies were served to the audience by students. The wind was chilly on the Mount of Light. People sipped their lemonade while snuggling close to one another.

Finally the diplomas were awarded to the eighty-six graduates. One by one they marched up on the platform, received the valuable paper, shook hands with several school and community dignitaries, and returned to their seats, properly graduated from Prophet Elias High School.

In my role as school president, I shook hands with each one of these precious young people. Next year, I thought, there will be one hundred and twenty graduates. *O God, the living stones of Galilee, bright, beautiful, and vibrant, are beginning to build their own hope and their own future.*

The February court appearance had been postponed until June. The June appearance was postponed again. Friends had helped me obtain postponements, because if I were to appear, I would be fined large amounts of money and run the risk of an order to demolish the unfinished building.

As I write this chapter, I have not yet appeared in court. In the meantime, I have met with literally hundreds of Israeli officials, including representatives from Prime Minister Shamir's office. The struggle for the building permit continues now into the summer of 1990. Every day there are conversations, meetings, hopes, and disappointments.

Prophet Elias High School is jammed with 850 students from twenty-one villages. The students—Christians, Muslims, and Druze—taught by a faculty of fifty, including two Jewish teachers, occupy every corner in the original building and the finished classrooms in the extension. Still more parents, more villages in Galilee, call to ask if their children can come to our school. The Ministry of Education has given us a new quota rating of 95.5 percent, one of the highest in all Israel, based on our students' high test scores and the variety of technological classes we offer. We have also received approval to develop a community college on our campus, the first in any Arab Palestinian village and the first in all of Galilee. These accolades and approvals, however, do not get us the vital building permit, which is issued only through the Ministry of Interior Affairs.

The permit will come, of that I am sure. The future will be what we want it to be, if we do not give up, if we are steadfast in the face of the pressures against us in the Jewish Israeli community and even among some poor collaborators in our Palestinian community. We know that what we are trying to do is right.

We want to improve the social, educational, and economic status of the Palestinians in Galilee, but more important, we are working to create a mentality of self-reliance among our people, a mentality of nonviolent struggle for human rights. We need to create a new reality in Galilee, changing the situation from injustice and inequality between Palestinians and Jews to a true partnership of equals. Never can the roles simply be reversed, the Palestinians becoming the lords or conquerors of the Jews. It is a matter of building bridges among members of the same family. Always there is the temptation of violence and might, but the ones who build bridges acknowledge, "My friend is also right, and I am also wrong."

This is to become Godlike. God cares for the oppressed and feels their torment and suffering. In these struggles God always takes the side of liberation, not the side of particular people or nations as favorites. God also calls to the oppressor to be liberated from fear, anger, and lust for power.

This land, this Palestine, this Israel, does not belong to either Jews or Palestinians. Rather, we are compatriots who belong to the land and to each other. If we cannot live together, we surely will be buried here together. We must choose life.

Abuna Chacour continues to be the Melkite parish priest in Ibillin. His mailing address is P.O. Box 102, Ibillin, Galilee, 30012, Israel.

Notes

Chapter 2: We Don't Want You Here!
1. From a personal statistical project done by Abuna Chacour in 1968–69 while studying at Hebrew University. Chacour also learned that approximately 350,000 Palestinian Christians lived in Australia, Canada, the United States, Europe, and in refugee camps in the Middle East in the late 1960s.

Chapter 3: The Tree Must Live!
1. Sabri Jiryis, *The Arabs in Israel* (New York: Monthly Review Press, 1976), 295. Table 5, "Land Lost by Some Arab Villages in Israel Between 1945–1962," indicates that Ibillin (Ablin) had 16, 019 dunums in 1945, and 10,206 dunums in 1962. In 1989, the village estimated it had lost approximately 70 percent of its land.

Chapter 4: Palm Sunday Prisoners
1. The bishop's name is from the Christian tradition in the village. According to Latin sources, a bishop from Zebulon was one of nineteen bishops from Palestine who attended the Council of Nicea. See *Spicilegium Solesmense*, edited by Jean-Baptiste Pitra (Paris: Unveranderter Abdruck, 1852; new edition, Graz, Austria: Akademische Druck, U. Verlagsanstalt, 1962), 531.

Chapter 5: A New Jeremiah Speaks
1. Rosemary Radford Ruether and Herman J. Ruether, *The Wrath of Jonah: The Crisis of Religious Nationalism in the Israeli-Palestinian Conflict* (San Francisco: Harper & Row, 1989), 133.
2. Jiryis, *Arabs in Israel*, 94–96.

Chapter 8: We Young Priests
1. Israel Shahak, "Arab Villages Destroyed in Israel: A Report," in *Documents from Israel* (London: Ithaca Press, 1975), 47.

2. Ian Lustik, *Arabs in the Jewish State: Israel's Control of a National Minority* (Austin: University of Texas Press, 1980), 63–64.

Chapter 9: Escape
1. Helena Cobban, *The Palestinian Liberation Organisation: People, Power, and Politics* (Cambridge: Cambridge University Press, 1984), 51–52.

Chapter 10: Of Cucumbers, Books, and Pigs
1. See Lustik, *Arabs in the Jewish State*, 169–82, for a full discussion of the Israeli laws and policies regarding the seizure of Arab land in Israel.
2. Jiryis, *Arabs in Israel*, 295.
3. Ibid., 80–81.
4. Ibid., 76, 79.
5. Joseph L. Ryan, S.J., "Refugees Within Israel: The Case of the Villagers of Kafr Bir'im and Iqrit," *Journal of Palestine Studies* 2 (Summer 1973): 7–8.
6. Ibid.
7. Ibid., 8.
8. Ibid., 9; Father Yusef Istephan, in his memoirs, *My Testimony* (privately published, 1986), 69; Jiryis, *Arabs in Israel*, 92.
9. "Nobody Will Say How the Piggies Go to Market," Part 1 of "Pigs and the Law," *Jerusalem Post*, June 26, 1985.
10. "Producer: Israel Has Over One Million Pork-eaters," Part 4 of "Pigs and the Law," *Jerusalem Post*, July 5, 1985.

Chapter 11. Marching in Jerusalem
1. Ruether and Ruether, *Wrath of Jonah*, 135–36.
2. "Return of Bir'im, Ikrit Villagers 'Impossible'," *Jerusalem Post*, August 9, 1972.
3. "Greek Catholics Skip Sunday Services," *Jerusalem Post*, August 14, 1972.
4. "Raya Leads 2,000 in March in Jerusalem," *Jerusalem Post*, August 24, 1972.

Chapter 14.: We Are Human Beings, Not Cattle or Insects
1. "Tree Planting Stopped in Bir'im," *Jerusalem Post*, February 18, 1979.

Chapter 16: Remember the Little Ones, My Son
1. Lustik, *Arabs in the Jewish State*, 168–69.
2. Ibid., 189–92.

3. Ibid., 195.

Chapter 18: The Mount of Light
1. Lustik, *Arabs in the Jewish State,* 194.
2. Ibid., 195.
3. Jiryis, *Arabs in Israel,* 105–6.
4. Ibid., 77, 80.

Chapter 19: For Sale: One Permit
1. Cobban, *The Palestinian Liberation Organisation,* 128–30.

Chapter 20: Betrayed
1. Jimmy Carter, *The Blood of Abraham: Insights into the Middle East* (Boston: Houghton Mifflin, 1985), 96.
2. "Shamir Leads Israelis at Haddad's Funeral," *Jerusalem Post,* January 17, 1984.

Chapter 22: Crucified in Gaza
1. Meron Benvenisti, *The West Bank Handbook: A Political Lexicon* (Jerusalem: Jerusalem Post, 1986), 137.
2. "15 Dead in Only One Week of Uprising," *Al Fajr* newspaper, East Jerusalem, February 14, 1988. Khader's birthdate was August 8, 1968, according to his family.
3. Benvenisti, *West Bank Handbook,* 91–92.
4. *Statistical Abstract of Israel 1988* (Jerusalem: Central Bureau of Statistics, 1988), 705. The 1987 population figure for Gaza was 564.1 thousand. Using the stated projected annual increase of 3.4 percent, population figures can be estimated as follows: 1988—583.3 thousand; 1989—603.1 thousand; 1990—623.6 thousand.
5. Sara Roy, *The Gaza Strip Survey* (Jerusalem: Jerusalem Post, 1986), 1.
6. The Reverend Don Wagner, "Crucified in Gaza," prepared privately for the Palestine Human Rights Campaign, Chicago. The detailed article was written after an extensive interview with Khader's father in Gaza City on February 19, 1988, eleven days after his son's death. The account in this book is a compilation of information from Abuna Chacour's visit with Khader's mother in March 1988 and Wagner's interview with Khader's father.

Glossary

Key: A = Arabic; H = Hebrew; G = Greek; F = French

Abu (A): father; used as a loving, familiar title with the name of the man's oldest son—for example, Abu Rudah, literally "father of Rudah"

Abuna (A): literally "our father"; loving, familiar title for a Christian priest

Ahlan Wassahlan (A): "Welcome!"

Allahu Akbar (A): "God is great"; used in the Muslim call to prayer

Dunum (A): a measure of land; four dunums equal approximately one acre

Eretz Yisrael (H): literally "land of Israel," name given to the state of Israel; some nationalists extend this name to the West Bank and Gaza Strip

Gaza Strip: narrow strip of land, twenty-eight miles long by five miles wide, alongside the Mediterranean Sea, bordered by Egypt to the south, Israel to the east and north; administered by Egypt 1948–67; occupied by Israel since 1967

Icon (G): an image or picture of Jesus, Mary, or a saint, usually painted on wood, sometimes adorned with silver or gold

Iconostasis (G): a partition or screen decorated with icons, separating the altar area from the rest of the church

Intifada (A): the Palestinian struggle for freedom in the West Bank and Gaza Strip

Jabal el Ghoul (A): Mountain of the Ogre, or Monster, located in Galilee

211

Jabal Ennuur (A): Mountain of Light, the new name for Jabal el Ghoul

Keffiyeh (A): a cloth headdress worn by Arab men as a protection against dust and heat; a large square of cotton cloth, draped and folded, held in place by a cord wound about the head

Kibbutz (H): Jewish collective farm

Knesset (H): Israel's single-chamber parliament, which has 120 elected deputies

Laissez passer (F): a pass authorizing access to or travel in a place or country

Melkite (A): a Byzantine church in communion with the Roman Catholic church

Mère (F): mother

Muezzin (A): the singer who summons people to pray in the mosque

Occupied Palestine: the areas of the West Bank and Gaza Strip declared as the modern Palestine, November 15, 1988; Palestine is militarily occupied by Israel

Père (F): father

Salaam Alekhum (A): "Peace be with you all"

Sheikh (A): Muslim clergyman

Ululate: to emit a high-pitched, continuous cry with a wavering tone, produced by rapidly touching the tongue to the roof of the mouth; ululations are usually done by women on occasions of great joy or sorrow

Um (A): mother; used as a loving, familiar title with the name of the woman's oldest son—for example, Um Rudah, literally "mother of Rudah"

West Bank: a kidney-shaped area of land lying to the west of the Jordan River, with an area of about 2,200 square miles, or about 22 percent of the original Palestine; attached to Jordan after the 1948 war, then occupied by Israel after the 1967 war